TO:
Elle

FROM: Sahra

Abte ~~Sire~~

DATE:
Aug 21, 2018

PRAISE FOR

Brave Beauty

"Getting started with a private devotional time when you are young is the key to a lifelong habit of spending daily time with God. Lynn Cowell turns a big task into mini-chapters and easily digestible moments of time spent with God. It's my heart's desire that every girl learns *Brave Beauty*!"

DANNAH GRESH, bestselling author and
creator of Secret Keeper Girl

"I cannot begin to tell you how important this book is for girls. As I read through the pages, I found myself approaching every word with excitement and anticipation, even desiring to take the chapter quizzes and participate in the journaling! If you have a young girl in your life, I beg you to get this for her. Girls' lives will be divinely changed because of *Brave Beauty*."

SHARI BRAENDEL, author of **Help Me
Jesus, I Have Nothing to Wear!** and
president of Fashion Meets Faith

"*Brave Beauty* is just what young girls need at a critical time in life! These are one hundred bite-sized pieces of godly encouragement from a trusted voice. I'll definitely be using in our home!"

COURTNEY DEFEO, author of **In This
House, We Will Giggle**

faithgirlz™

BRAVE BEAUTY

FINDING THE FEARLESS YOU

LYNN COWELL

 ZONDER**kidz**

ZONDERKIDZ

Brave Beauty
Copyright © 2017 by Lynn Cowell

This title is also available as a Zondervan ebook.

Requests for information should be addressed to:
Zonderkidz, 3900 Sparks Dr. SE, Grand Rapids, Michigan 49546

ISBN 978-0-310763147

Author is represented by the literary agency of The Fedd Agency, Inc., P. O.
Box 341973, Austin, Texas 78734

Zonderkidz is a trademark of Zondervan.

Interior design: Denise Froehlich

Printed in the United States of America

17 18 19 20 21 /LSC/ 10 9 8 7 6 5 4 3 2 1

CONTENTS

I'm Beautiful

SECTION 2—I AM BRAVE
I Can Be Me

I Can Stand Alone

I Can Do the Scary Things

I Can Change

I Can Redefine Beautiful

I Am Brave Enough to Believe

I Am Truthful

I Can Do It Scared

SECTION 3—I AM CONFIDENT

My Family

You Are with Me

I Can Stand Up for Others

I Can Overcome

I Can Be Part of a Chain of Courage

I Can Be Brave Even When I Am in over My Head

I Can Build Myself Up

I Can Confidently Move Forward

I Can Know He Is Always with Me

DEDICATION

To my niece, Carley
You are both brave and beautiful.
Thank you so much for all of
your help with **Brave Beauty**
and making time to spend with
your Aunt Lynn. I love you!

INTRODUCTION

Hey there! My name is Lynn and I'm crazy excited that you're joining me through *Brave Beauty*. Do you like to be adventurous? I do! I love to go places I've never been, do things I've never done and see things I've never seen. Sometimes, though, my adventures take bravery . . . a lot of bravery! You know what else? I'm not always brave, but I want to be. I don't want to miss all the exciting things God has for me and I've discovered that to do that, I need to be brave.

That's what the next "100 moments" are all about. Whether you plan to use this book for 100 days, a 100 weeks or anything in between, we're going on a journey to learn to become courageous, confident, and fearless.

Confident. It's a big word. Dictionary.com explains its meaning as: full trust; belief in the powers, trustworthiness, or reliability of a person or thing. That is who we want to become. Girls who have full trust, belief in the powers, trustworthiness, and reliability of Christ.

Growing up. I don't have to tell you that life can be tough. You already know that. Maybe people around you like your mom, a teacher, or a coach are helping you figure out all these changes. Or maybe, you feel like you're doing it alone. You don't really know what you're doing. I get that. I often feel like I don't know what I'm doing too; I think it is part of being human. I have found some things that help me when I don't know what to do next and one might really surprise you. I found it by accident.

Writing. Yes, writing! I'm guessing that so far in your life, writing is something you have done mostly at school. Assignments. Homework-type stuff. Writing and fun—to you, those two just don't belong in the same sentence!

When I was in third grade, someone gave me a little, gold book that said, "Five Year Diary" on the outside. I can't even remember who gave me my first diary. I wish I did so I could thank them. I still have that little book, although it's a bit beat-up. (You can see it on my scrapbook. Just ask your parent if you can go to LynnCowell.com and click on "Brave Beauty". You'll find my scrapbook there). When it was new, this book was filled with blank pages just waiting for me to record my thoughts and feelings.

If you were here, sitting with me around my big, round kitchen table, having a giant piece of double chocolate, chocolate chip Bundt cake (my favorite), I'd run up to my room, take my diary out of my drawer, and share with you some of those thoughts and feelings that filled up all the pages of that little book.

For many years, I kept all those words hidden. (I would have freaked out if anyone found it! Goodness, can you imagine? *Gasp!* All my secrets were stored there!) Inside was my heart; what I didn't want anyone else to know: having a crush on Jim *and* John, how I hoped one day to be a children's book illustrator, and how I liked my

summer until one of my best friends made me feel forgotten. Then I couldn't wait for summer to end.

I discovered that writing helped me figure out this
thing called becoming me. That's why I wrote this book;
I wanted to help you on this journey to becoming you; a
brave and fearless you!

Together, we're going to:

- See who God says you are
- Talk about tough stuff you're going through
- Look at people in the Bible and see how they handled hard
  things
- Get to know more about God and how He can help us
- Learn how His words can help us become fearless and
  brave.
- We'll have fun, too! Think of this book a bit like my little,
  gold diary.

Since writing in my diary was a big thing for me when I
was your age, I thought maybe you might try writing, too. That's
why I peppered quizzes and questions throughout this book. I
want you to think of it as a diary of sorts; a place where you can
write down your innermost thoughts; things you want to be just
between you and God. Who knows? Maybe like me, you'll hang
onto this book and one day read it when you're a grown up, too.

As you write, remember there are no right or wrong answers.
These answers are for your eyes only; not your parent, small
group leader, or anyone else. Just you!

I hope you like quizzes. I know that often these types of quizzes end with you adding up a score and the score telling you all

about who you are. Not these! I don't want you to put yourself into a box. These quizzes are just to get you thinking about you, who you are, what you like and what you don't like. It's the first step to you becoming confident in the girl God made you to be!

We'll wrap up each chapter with a Courageous Call, which simply means we will end each chapter with a call out to God to help us become fearless and brave; a prayer. You will notice that I end each prayer with "In Jesus' name, Amen." When Jesus was on earth, He told us, "And I will do whatever you ask in my name, so that the Father may be glorified in the Son." John 14:13 (NIV) What an amazing promise.

I really want you to feel like you have a friend in me, so on my website, I've created a scrapbook of pictures. Here you can see my diary and many of the other things I talk about in *Brave Beauty*. To find my scrapbook, just go to www.LynnCowell.com and click on "books". You'll see the *Brave Beauty* tab there where my scrapbook can be found.

Ready? I sure am. Let's go!

SECTION 1

I AM LOVED

CHAPTER 1

BELONGING TO GOD'S FAMILY

salvation, forgiveness, faith

Through *Brave Beauty,* we will take turns sharing things about one another, so hopefully you can feel like we are becoming friends.

Let's begin with when we were born.

My big entrance into this world took place at Allen Hospital in Waterloo, Iowa. (Want to know a crazy thing? My husband was born there too!) God made me part of a really big family. I was the seventh child of what would become eight; my parents' fifth daughter.

What do you know about the day you were born? Maybe you've heard the story many times or maybe you know very little about this important day. Share a few details in the space below.

Have pc that have red glowing
eyes Born St Joes Hospital in
Tac. WA. on Aug 21, 2008 -
I was my moms first born.

One thing that is true for both of us: we didn't get to pick any details surrounding *how* we came into this world. We didn't pick our parents or where and when our birth took place. We had no choice.

There is another "birth" that I did choose however, and so can you!

God also has a great, big family. The Bible tells us that we are not automatically born into His family, but we can be adopted into it.

Maybe you grew up learning about being a part of God's family. My mom taught me that I could be "adopted" by God, so when I was eight years old, I asked Him to make me His daughter.

Have you already asked God to make you a part of His family? If so, how wonderful! We're sisters. If you haven't yet, you can simply ask God to make you His child and you, too, will belong.

Let's end with a quiz that might help you get to know yourself just a little bit better.

GETTING TO KNOW YOU

(*Circle an answer below each question.*)

Can you remember when you first heard about Jesus?

a. I've been learning about Him for as long as I can remember.

b. I've just gotten to know Jesus. I'm reading this book so I can learn more.

c. This is all new to me.

How does becoming a part of a new family, God's family, make you feel?

a. Since I've always known, I don't really have any feelings at all.

b. I'm really excited! Being a part of God's family sounds fun.

c. I'm nervous because I don't understand it all.

Like my mom shared with me, have you had others tell you how they became a part of God's family?

a. Yes, I have heard many stories and they invited me to join too.

b. Yes, I heard their story but I didn't know I could become a part of God's family as well.

c. No, this is the first time I have heard this good news.

COURAGEOUS CALL

Dear God, being a part of Your family sounds so exciting! I want to learn more. Please help me to understand all the new things I'm going to learn about You. In Jesus' name, Amen.

CHAPTER 2

A DIFFERENT BIRTH

salvation, forgiveness, faith

There was a man in the Bible named Nicodemus, who felt a little confused. He heard about Jesus and saw miracles Jesus was doing, but he didn't really understand who Jesus was. He decided to go directly to Jesus and ask Him to explain.

Nicodemus was a leader in the church, but that didn't mean he had all the answers. Maybe that's why he visited Jesus at night. He may have been afraid someone might see him. He could have been fearful someone might make fun of him and think he was weird for talking to Jesus. Whatever his reason, Nicodemus was brave to approach Jesus in person with his questions.

The first thing Nicodemus wanted to know was who Jesus really was.

Have you ever been stumped by a riddle? I think Nicodemus might have thought Jesus was telling him a riddle when Jesus said, ". . . no one can see the kingdom of God unless they are born again." John 3:3 (NIV)

Now Nicodemus was even more confused than when he came. He asked Jesus, "How can a man be born again when he is already old? He cannot get inside his mother's body again!"

Jesus explained to Nicodemus he could *choose* to become a part of God's family.

Jesus shared that when God's son, Jesus, came to earth, He made it possible for all of Nicodemus's sins to be forgiven. Then he could become a part of God's family and join God in heaven one day.

Jesus explained it this way, "For this is how God loved the world: He gave his one and only Son, so that everyone who believes in him will not perish but have eternal life." John 3:16 (NLT)

You and I don't have to give God anything in exchange for our forgiveness; it's a gift. Even though we make mistakes every single day, the price of our sins has already been paid. Jesus did that for you and me! We simply accept God's forgiveness as a gift from Him. It's a gift He gave us because He loves us so much.

BECOMING BRAVE

Maybe like Nicodemus, you feel afraid others might think you are not smart because you don't know very much about Jesus. You may be scared that some might think you are weird if they find out you are a part of God's family; call you a goody-goody. I understand; I've had those feelings and I have had that happen. The more we get to know Jesus and understand who He is, the braver we will become.

COURAGEOUS CALL

Dear Jesus, I know not everyone chooses to be a part of Your family. I also know that I want to learn more about Your love for me. Give me courage, Jesus, not to worry about what others think. In Jesus' name, Amen.

CHAPTER 3

BECOMING ADOPTED

salvation, forgiveness, faith, family

D o you know anyone who is adopted? Maybe that someone is you.

When a family decides to adopt a child, they make that choice because they have a lot of love in their hearts and they want to share that love. Giving love makes them happy.

That is why God has decided to adopt us. The Bible explains it this way: "God decided in advance to adopt us into his own family by bringing us to himself through Jesus Christ. This is what he wanted to do, and it gave him great pleasure." Ephesians 1:5 (NLT)

God made the choice, way before you were born, that He wanted you to be a part of this big family of God. Having you in His family would make Him really happy and make you happy too!

Maybe you wonder why being in His family would make you happy. There are a lot of advantages to being in God's family.

When God is our father, He makes promises to us that He always keeps.

One of those promises is that He will never leave us or forsake us. Deuteronomy 31:6 says, "So be strong and courageous! Do not be afraid and do not panic before them. For the LORD your God will personally go ahead of you. He will neither fail you nor abandon you." (NLT) Part of becoming brave and fearless is knowing that we can be brave, because God is always with us.

As our father, God also shows compassion for us. He understands you when you are sad, even if no one else does. He is a tender father. Psalm 103:13 says it this way, "The LORD is like a father to his children, tender and compassionate to those who fear him." (NLT)

As our father, God promises to take care of our needs. (Matthew 6:32) He already knows the things we need and He will take care of those needs.

Best of all is God's love for us as His children. I love this verse: "See what great love the Father has lavished on us, that we should be called children of God! And that is what we are!" 1 John 3:1 (NIV) I know that word "lavished" is a big word, but it is one worth learning. It means to give in great amounts without limit. Yahoooo! How wonderful to be loved like that, in great amounts and without any limit. As God's children, that is how He loves us.

Now you know, there are many reasons to choose to be a part of God's great family.

BECOMING BRAVE

Today, ask someone you know who loves God to share with you their story of how they became part of God's great family.

COURAGEOUS CALL

Dear God, I can see it! You are a good father and You love me so much. Thank you for this love and the invitation You are giving to me. In Jesus' name, Amen.

CHAPTER 4

IT'S UP TO YOU

salvation, forgiveness, faith

Do you feel like you get to make a whole lot of decisions? Maybe or maybe not.

Someone else may tell you when you have to get up, do your homework, or go to bed. Maybe other people decide **when** and **what** you are going to eat. You may or may not get to make a choice when it comes to the clothes you buy, what you get to wear, and when. If you share a bedroom, you may have to compromise when it comes to decorating it. I'm guessing you may not have the option as to whether or not you have to clean your room on occasion. When you go to a restaurant, you probably do not have the power to select anything you want off the menu.

This can be extremely frustrating, I know! But at your age, you are well on your way to figuring out what is best for you and probably beginning to make some of these decisions on your own.

Here is the great news: there is only one person who can make the choice of whether you are going to be a part of God's family or not . . . and that person is definitely you—and ONLY you!

God gives every person, including you, the ability to make a choice. You can choose to be in God's family. You can decide whether or not you obey Him and experience His blessings. This decision is completely yours. Your mom can't do it for you. Neither can your dad, your sister, your pastor, or your friend. Only you can be the one brave enough to say, "Yes, God, I want to give up running my life and choose to let the one who knows me best call the shots instead."

I've made that decision and it has been the very best decision I ever made. I'm a part of God's family and I want you to be a part of it too. If that is what you want as well, just tell God and ask Him to make you His child.

BECOMING BRAVE

Have you ever told God thank you for sending Jesus to die for you? You can do that right now. You can tell Him thank you, ask Him to take away your sin just like He died to do, and start a relationship with you. If you need a little help with what to say, look at the prayer in the Courageous Call for today.

COURAGEOUS CALL

Dear Jesus, what You did for me was big—just to prove to me that You loved me. Thank you! Please take away my sin; forgive me. Thank you for loving me. I want to spend my life loving You back. In Jesus' name, Amen.

My Worth

CHAPTER 5

GETTING TO KNOW YOU

*getting to know yourself, be yourself,
purpose, self-worth, value, family*

Remember my diary? I think it's fun reading about who I was when I was younger. You know what I learned when I read it? I like me! Really . . . I was pretty cool.

I wish now that I could go back and tell me just how cool I was, because I really didn't know. I worried a lot about friends, parties, and not doing the things I knew were wrong and whether or not I was going to turn out ok. I struggled with liking myself just the way I was, especially if I thought someone else didn't like me. I didn't always feel good about myself and had a hard time being brave enough to just be myself.

Maybe when I talked about my struggles you thought, "Me too!" You worry about fitting in because in some ways you are just a bit different than others. Your personality, body, even your family isn't the same as others so sometimes you have a hard time liking yourself just the way you are.

You know what? You don't have to be like me! In fact, if you were like me, you would not fully be you. You can **know** now that you are already amazing. When God created you, He made you great from the very beginning.

He says about us in Zephaniah 3:17 (NIV), "The LORD your God is with you, the Mighty Warrior who saves. He will take great delight in you; in his love he will no longer rebuke you, but will rejoice over you with singing."

You know why He is singing?

Ever listen to love songs? Why do guys and girls write all that mushy stuff? It's because they are crazy about someone! They are so in love; they just have to sing about them.

That is how Jesus feels about you. He is absolutely crazy about you! Knowing for sure that He is crazy about us can fill up all those doubting places in our vulnerable hearts. That's when we can be ok with ourselves just the way we are.

Let's learn a little more about what makes amazing you, so amazing!

GETTING TO KNOW YOU

(Circle at least one answer below each question.)

On a Saturday afternoon, would you: (It's ok to pick more than one!)

a. Read a book by yourself.
b. Paint your nails with your best friend.
c. Go exploring in the woods with a group of buddies.

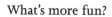

What's more fun?

a. Writing a drama while your
   imagination dreams away.

b. A sleepover with your two favorite friends.

c. A party with a pile of girls.

How do you feel about meeting new people?

a. I like the friends I have. I don't really need more.

b. A new friend now and then is fun.

c. New friends? The more, the better!

COURAGEOUS CALL

Dear Jesus, thank you that You "take great delight in me." Wow! That is really cool. Thank you for letting me know that I am that special to You! In Jesus' name, Amen.

My Worth

CHAPTER 6

NEVER HIDDEN

purpose, self-worth, value

Have you ever had someone act like they knew all about you, but they really didn't? Maybe *that* was super obvious from the last birthday gift they gave you. In fact, you really didn't know how to react when you opened the gift. But I'm sure you let them know you appreciated them thinking of you no matter what they gave you.

Maybe it wasn't their fault that they didn't know you very well. Maybe they don't get to spend a lot of time with you. It could be they didn't know what to get you because while you are trying to figure out who you really are; the personality you show to others keeps changing.

You know someone who does know you well? Perfectly, in fact?

God!

Psalm 139:1 (NIV) tells us: "You have searched me, LORD, and you know me."

These words were written by David. You may have heard of him: shepherd boy turned king? When Samuel the prophet came to David's home to choose a king from all of his dad's sons, David's dad didn't even call him in from the field where he was watching sheep. He was overlooked by his dad. Maybe, because he spent so much time away from his family and out in the fields, his family didn't really see the man David was becoming. Fighting off lions and bears in order to protect the sheep he was watching, they didn't see the brave person he was growing up to be. Because they didn't see, they didn't really know.

But God did. God "searched" for David. He knew the man this boy was growing into and He made sure David was brought in from the field when Samuel came to anoint the next king. Though he was the youngest, he was the one chosen.

God knows you because He has taken the time to search you.

The word "search" here in the Bible means, "to look carefully in order to find something hidden."

That is what God did with David. David may have been hidden out of the sight of his dad and brothers, out in the field alone watching the sheep. But he was not hidden from God! While David was watching sheep, God was watching him. God saw the courageous character David was developing while out in the field.

That is what God has done and is doing every day with you! He is looking carefully at **you** to discover everything there is to know about you.

Why would the Creator of the universe do that? It's because He loves you. He never gets bored knowing everything there is to know about you.

It makes me really happy to know that someone enjoys me that much. How about you?

BECOMING BRAVE

What is some thing about you that hardly anyone knows? Share a few things here. Thank God that He knows this secret part of you and that He wants to know even more about you! God is the best secret-keeper there is; He knows and understands your heart, because He created it.

_____

_____

_____

_____

COURAGEOUS CALL

Dear God, knowing that You want to know everything about me makes me feel special. Thank you so much. In Jesus' name, Amen.

CHAPTER 7

PRICELESS

family, self-worth, friends

Iwill never outgrew fairy tales. I know; at some point a girl is supposed to stop reading and watching them. But I haven't.

There is something about me, this mostly tomboy girl, that once in a while likes to take in a story about a princess.

Several years ago in England, a real prince and princess, Prince William and Princess Kate, were married. It was such a huge affair and really cool to see! (You can see some of it on YouTube if your mom or dad says that's okay.)

One of the most beautiful things Princess Kate wore that day was her headpiece. The news said it was made of all diamonds and when they described its value they said it was priceless. That means they could not even say how much money it would cost if someone wanted to buy it—it is just worth too much!

Did you know that is what God says about you?

Here is what he says in Isaiah 43:3, 4 "I paid a huge price for you: . . . *That's* how much you mean to me! *That's* how much I love you! I'd sell off the whole world to get you back, trade the creation just for you." (The Message)

God says **you** are worth more to Him than the entire world. He says you are priceless! He paid a huge price for you when He sent His only son, Jesus, to come to earth to die for you. That is how He proved to you your worth.

It's easy for us to get caught up in the idea that things are important. Every day we hear about a new this thing and a great that thing we should get. But did you notice in this verse what God says is priceless? He says it is a person; you. *People* are priceless to Him.

It takes bravery to be a girl who thinks people are more important than things. The culture we live in makes "stuff" like clothes and the newest phone so important. A brave beauty recognizes that people are more important than things. Since this thinking isn't "normal" in our culture, to think and act differently, you are going to have to fight against the thinking that things are more important than people.

There are going to be days when you don't *feel* all that priceless. Someone might say hurtful or embarrassing words to you at school, at a party, or in another social setting. An adult may take their anger out on you and say things that leave you aching inside. Please remember: other people's words do not diminish the truth that every one of us is more precious than rubies. You have to be your own best friend and tell yourself the truth—you are worth everything to Jesus.

BECOMING BRAVE

Start winning this brave battle today by listing five people in your life who are priceless to you. If you're really brave, list ten. Now, let them know. You could give them a call, write them a note, or send a text. Any way, to let them know they are priceless to you!

_____

_____

_____

_____

COURAGEOUS CALL

Dear Jesus, thank you for seeing in me a value that I sometimes have a hard time seeing myself. Thank you for creating me and treating me as priceless! In Jesus' name, Amen.

CHAPTER 8

YOU'VE ALREADY GOT IT

self-worth, value, hurt

I knew exactly the way it was going to go down every time we picked teams in gym class. Jimmy and I would be dead last. I couldn't throw a ball for anything and Jimmy ran slower than the rest of us. I often felt like I just didn't have what it takes. I wasn't very athletic. I often struggled with math problems. I couldn't play the piano anything like my sister.

What was I good at? What could I do well?

Recently I found this verse in a book in the Bible called Hebrews: "May he equip you with all you need for doing his will. May he produce in you, through the power of Jesus Christ, every good thing that is pleasing to him. All glory to him forever and ever! Amen." Hebrews 13:21 (NLT)

Did you read that? God has given us, you and me, all we need for doing His will. He knew all along that I didn't need to be a whiz in math; I needed to be great in English! The pressure to have to be great at everything is off because God didn't make me to do everything. He has given me everything I need to do what He wants me to do. The same is true for you.

You might not be great at sports or music, but you can figure out any math problem. Reading might be really difficult for you, but just look and see what you can do with colored pencils. Writing? You have a hard time putting into words what you are trying to say, but you feel free when you are running on a field.

That is great! You **do** you! Remember, no one else can be you. Only **you** can do what you do exactly the way you do it. We are not all the same and that is more than ok. It is exactly the way God planned it. He made it so that we need each other. I need your gifts and you need mine. How wonderful is that?

BECOMING BRAVE

As we learn more about who God says we are—accepted, loved, and chosen—we can choose to become brave and help others know who God says they are. Look for someone around you who might not know who God says they are. Take one step today to being a friend to them. Ask them to sit by you at lunch, choose them to do a project with you, or invite them to hang out one day after school.

COURAGEOUS CALL

Dear God, thank you for choosing to make each one of us different. Help me to recognize and celebrate the uniqueness of me, Lord. It makes me feel much better knowing You've given me everything I need to do what You have for me to do. That takes away my need to worry. I don't have to fear; You've taken care of it all. In Jesus' name, Amen.

I'm Accepted

CHAPTER 9

ACCEPTED

left out, friends, sad, hurt

Icouldn't think of anything I had done to make Janna **not** like me. We had some of the same friends and went to some of the same places together. Yes, I was sure of it. We were friends.

Trying not to make it obvious, I huddled in the corner and watched. *Would she have an invitation for me?* Janna hadn't invited me to her party last year, but this year we were better friends. Weren't we?

Yes; surely she would invite me this year. She wouldn't forget about me this time.

Suddenly I noticed she was done; there were no more invitations to hand out.

I guess we weren't such good friends after all.

It's times like this, when we feel left out, on the outside, forgotten, that we just want to hide. We don't understand; why would someone treat us this way? Why would they make us feel on the outside? We just want to be included like everyone else.

We want to be accepted.

Friend, there are going to be times when you are rejected by people. These can be the hardest moments to be brave. Our emotions want to ooze out everywhere; out our eyes through the tears we cry and out of our mouth through the words we say. The only place that can feel safe is on our beds, crying our eyes out.

These tough times are going to come; they just are! It's a part of life. Jesus even told us about them, ". . . In this world you will have trouble. But take heart! I have overcome the world." John 16:33 (NIV) There it is—so very plain—you will have trouble.

So if you know trouble is coming, the best thing you can do is get ready for it!

In the verse I just shared, I purposely left off the first part of what Jesus said. Before He talked about trouble He said, "I have told you these things, so that in me you may have peace."

Knowing Jesus' words can give us peace even when trouble is coming. When we learn what the Bible says about us, we can speak these words to our heart when it is hurting. Knowing He accepts us heals our hurts when others reject us. We become brave when we turn to Him with our hurts instead of turning against those who hurt us.

GETTING TO KNOW YOU

(Circle at least one answer below each question.)

What types of things can make you feel rejected? (You can pick more than one.)

a. When teams are chosen at school.

b. When you see pictures of friends hanging out that you are not a part of.

c. When others make plans without you.

When you feel left out, what do you usually do?

a. Talk to one of my parents.

b. Cry by myself.

c. Do something else to keep myself busy.

How do you feel about Jesus saying "in this world you will have trouble"?

a. I know troubles can help me to grow stronger.

b. I wish it wasn't true.

c. I pretend I don't have any troubles.

COURAGEOUS CALL

Dear Jesus, I don't like that troubles are a part of life, but there is no getting around it. Please help me to prepare my mind and heart so that when it comes, I can respond bravely. In Jesus' name, Amen.

I'm Accepted

CHAPTER 10

SISTERS

left out, friends, sad, hurt, family, loving difficult people

If you have siblings, then you know just how hard it can be at times not to fight with them. I should know; I have seven! Most of the time, the things we fought about were silly.

There was a set of sisters in the Bible and the thing they fought about wasn't silly. In Genesis we meet a brave sister named Leah. When the Bible describes her it says: "Leah had weak eyes." Genesis 29:17 (NIV) I don't know about you, but I wouldn't want to be described that way!

Leah had a sister named Rachel. The Bible calls Rachel "lovely," which was a huge bummer for Leah. A guy named Jacob worked for their dad. Jacob was in love with Rachel. But Laban, the girls' dad, wanted Leah to get married first because she was the oldest and that was their culture's tradition. Jacob wasn't in love with Leah, though. He only wanted the lovely Rachel.

Laban pulled a trick on Jacob and got Jacob to marry Leah first. Jacob was furious! So who does Jacob take his anger out on? Poor Leah. Jacob rejects her, making it clear he loves Rachel.

Leah really struggles with feeling rejected. She keeps trying to do everything she can, having more and more sons to get Jacob to love her. Nothing works. Finally, after trying and trying to get Jacob to care for her, she realizes nothing is going to work. No matter what she does, it doesn't change Jacob's heart toward her.

Finally, Leah changes the person she is looking to for the acceptance she wants so badly. "This time I will praise the Lord," Genesis 29:35 (NIV) she says.

It took Leah a long time to see that sometimes there is **nothing** we can do to get other people to like and accept us. Hoping to find that acceptance first in Jacob and then in her sons didn't work for Leah. When she started to see this, she turned to the Lord.

When we realize we don't have other people's approval and acceptance, but we do we have God's, we can be brave. We can be brave to keep on going and finding God's approval even when we don't have it from others.

Leah was brave **and** beautiful. Brave because she never quit believing God would help her. Even though the Bible said she had "weak eyes," I still think she was beautiful, because she set her eyes on Jesus.

BECOMING BRAVE

Like Leah, is there an area in your life you wish was different? Maybe you, too, feel hurt. Share it below. Your step today is to recognize that this may not get any better than it is now, but God will still help you through it. He can help you set your eyes on how much He accepts you and less on those who don't.

_____

_____

_____

_____

COURAGEOUS CALL

Dear God, no one likes to be hurt by other people. Help me, when it happens, to come to You first so You can heal my hurt. In Jesus' name, Amen.

I'm Accepted

CHAPTER 11

APPROVED

left out, friends, sad, hurt

I t was a sizzling hot summer in our city this year. Not only were the temperatures scalding, but there was no rain. Days and days went by without rain.

In the spring, the flowers in my yard had been gorgeous. The cool days and spring showers gave them everything they needed. All I had to do was look out my window and enjoy!

But as summer heated up, I just kept watching my plants. They began to droop from being so dry. Telling myself, *I'm too busy to go out and water*, I did nothing to help them. Eventually, many of my once-beautiful flowers died. They just couldn't keep going without what they needed.

Our hearts can be a bit like my flowers. When life is easy, it is not hard to wear a smile and be happy. But when things get hot and hard, it's a whole lot tougher.

Just as my flowers needed me to water and fertilize them, our hearts need the same. We need to take the time to give them what they need to keep going and what they need is the love of Jesus.

When we feel rejected, we have to remind ourselves the truth God says: you will forever and always be accepted by God! He puts it in writing in a letter that Paul, a follower of Jesus, wrote to some people called the Romans: "Accept one another, then, just as Christ accepted you, in order to bring praise to God." Romans 15:7 (NIV) The first part of this verse is important, but right now, I want you to skip that part.

Instead, read out loud the part between the two commas: just as Christ accepted you.

I kind of laughed a bit when I looked up the definition of the word accepted. Want to hear what it means? Generally approved; usually regarded as normal and right. Yes! (Fist pump here!) God says I'm normal just the way I am. He accepts me. He approves of me.

The same is true for you! You are normal. You are accepted, and He approves of you just the way you are.

So you know what this means for us?

I can accept me. I can approve of myself. You, too, can accept and approve of yourself. If the God of the universe says we're okay, then we can believe it.

Say this out loud: I am normal. I am approved. I am accepted!

BECOMING BRAVE

What do you think of yourself? God says He accepts you and approves of you. Do you accept and approve of yourself? Below write three things you like about yourself just the way you are. If you're really brave, write six.

COURAGEOUS CALL

Jesus, thank you so much for accepting and approving of me. Help me to really understand this so I change the way I see myself. Knowing You accept and approve of me gives me confidence. In Jesus' name, Amen.

You're Accepted

CHAPTER 12

CHOSEN

self-esteem, sad, bravery, value, friends, left out, friends, hurt

Even when I was in the smallest of small schools, I wasn't chosen.

Our class had those elections where the kids in your class get to pick a president, someone who would help the teacher pick the rules. It was never me; not in elementary, middle, or high school.

As I have gotten older, I've come to realize it's okay if people don't pick me. In fact, I've found out that sometimes it has been a good thing for me when I wasn't picked. Sometimes, when we're not picked, God is preparing us for something even more special or protecting us from something that otherwise might not be beneficial for us.

Elementary school was the first time I remember not being chosen. In fifth grade, I wasn't picked to be a part of our school's government. I felt so sad; I thought I would have been a great president.

Then, an opportunity came up at my church to be in a choir for young people. You know what I discovered? I was good at singing, really good in fact! That year they gave me a solo to sing in front of my whole church. (Want to hear something super crazy? That was the first time that the boy, who later became my husband, ever saw me. How wild is that!)

Here is what I wrote in my little gold diary that night: "Tonight we had the cantata. I had a solo. I was a little bit scared. It was great." (5th grade)

I'm not saying I wouldn't ever have met Greg if I weren't a part of that choir. I am saying that God may have allowed me to not be picked for government at my school, but He did make a way for me to be picked for something that eventually led to something even better. I ended up really enjoying singing and I became a part of many singing groups throughout my years in school.

God wants us to know that whether we are picked by people or not, we are always chosen by Him. Jesus says in John 15:16 (NLT), "You didn't choose me. I chose you. I appointed you to go and produce lasting fruit, so that the Father will give you whatever you ask for, using my name."

Friend, you have been picked. You are chosen.

BECOMING BRAVE

Say out loud: "I chose you." Now, write out John 15:16 on a piece of paper or card. Keep this reminder in a place where you can read it when you are feeling not so chosen: in your backpack, by your bed, or even as a note on your phone.

COURAGEOUS CALL

Dear Jesus, I love knowing You picked me; that I am chosen by You. On the days when friends don't pick me and I feel like they choose other people over me, please remind me that I am, and always will be, chosen by You. In Jesus' name, Amen.

My Changing Body

CHAPTER 13

HIS PERFECT ONE

self-worth, beauty, body changes

I had seen them before: pimples. Having six brothers and sisters become teenagers before me, I wasn't completely thrown off when these new, red things started showing up on my skin. I did **not**, however, like them. Would they go away? How long would they stay? Would everyone notice? All I knew was that they looked like flaws on my face.

Here's what I wrote in my diary from sixth grade: "I'm getting pimples all over my face! It must be because I'm 12! This is the pits!"

Maybe you aren't experiencing blemishes on your skin. You might be seeing other changes going on with your body and you're not quite sure how you feel about them.

You might look in the mirror and feel like all of these changes are happening way too fast or you might feel just the opposite. **When will I start to look like I'm growing up?**

Growing from a girl to a woman is not an easy process. It's going to require bravery!

I know it might be hard to believe, but God even has something to say about the way you look. Song of Solomon 5:2 (NIV) says you are "my treasure, my darling, my dove, my perfect one." Did you read that? He says you are His perfect one!

We'll dig more into this in our next chapter, but for now, know that what you see and what God sees might not be the same. He says you are beautiful just the way you are.

GETTING TO KNOW YOU:

(Circle one answer below each question.)

How do you feel about the changes that are happening or will be happening with your body?

a. I'm excited! I can't wait!

b. It doesn't really matter to me. I'm fine.

c. I wish I could stay a little girl forever.

Do you feel like you have enough information about your changing body?

a. I wish someone would tell me more of what I can expect.

b. I'll just take the changes as they come.

c. I don't want to talk about it; it scares me.

How do you feel about your appearance?

a. I like what I see in the mirror.

b. It's ok. I would like to think I'm prettier, but accept who I am.

c. I hope it gets better.

COURAGEOUS CALL

Dear Lord, help me as I am changing—on the inside and the outside. I know You made my body to do what it is about to do. Help me to not think it is weird and to trust that You know what You're doing. In Jesus' name, Amen.

CHAPTER 14

ABSOLUTELY FLAWLESS

self-worth, beauty, body changes

When my face first started breaking out, I know what I thought of myself and what other people thought of me. But I had no idea what God thought of me.

I wish I had. That would have changed everything.

It was much later in my life that I found this verse in Song of Solomon 4:7 (MSG): "You're beautiful from head to toe, my dear love, beautiful beyond compare, absolutely flawless."

I was shocked! Me? Beautiful? Absolutely flawless?

Here was the Bible telling me that just as I was, whatever I saw in the mirror, was perfect to God. My head and heart really needed to hear this.

There was nothing wrong with me.

You know those positive words you sometimes hear from your mom or dad, teacher, coaches, friends, and family? Take those to heart. Especially when the words are coming from those who love you so much. They aren't just speaking words. They love you and see the beauty of you. Can you imagine how much more magnified that love must be from the one who created you? It is literally beyond our ability to fully understand.

Friend, God made you beautiful. There is nothing wrong with me and there is nothing wrong with you. In fact, when you and I were made, before God did anything, He took a look at Himself. Yes, He looked at Himself and knew that He was very good. That is when He decided to make you and me like Him. Genesis 1:27 puts it this way: "So God created mankind in his own image, in the image of God he created them; male and female he created them." After he was all done, "God saw all that he had made, and it was very good." Genesis 1:31 (NIV) God was good and who He had made—us—was good too.

King David really understood just how good we are. He said to God: "I thank you because I am awesomely made, wonderfully; your works are wonders—I know this very well." Psalm 139:14 (CJB)

David spoke of the incredible process God went through to create us: "For you created my inmost being; you knit me together in my mother's womb," Psalm 139:13 (NIV) he wrote. While you were in your mother's body, God was busy choosing your nose, the color of your eyes, the exact shade of your skin, and creating the bones that would one day make up your height.

David was able to recognize how absolutely amazing our bodies are. It's time for us to recognize the beauty of how we are created as well.

BECOMING BRAVE

When you think of these words that the Bible uses to describe you—flawless, perfect, wonderfully made—how do you feel? Do you find this easy to believe or do you find you are struggling a bit?

_____

_____

_____

_____

COURAGEOUS CALL

Dear Jesus, thank you so much for making me me! I know that on the outside, I'm changing every day. Help me trust that all of the changes that are happening and are coming are good. In Jesus' name, Amen.

CHAPTER 15

BEAUTIFUL YOU

self-worth, beauty, body changes

I'm guessing that like me, there are days when you don't feel "beautiful from head to toe," "beautiful beyond compare," and "absolutely flawless." You may look in the mirror sometimes and struggle to thank God for what you see. That's ok; that's normal. There is a lot going on right now in your body and in your mind; you are growing from the girl you were into the women you are becoming. That process is not easy! Since this is not a simple time in your life, it is a time when you've got to help yourself out. Fearlessly discover yourself.

Your mind, right now, is trying to decide what to think about you. (I know this sounds kind of weird, but stick with me here.)

You—your mind, your heart, your body—are at a very important time of your life. Right now, you are making up your mind about what **you** think about you. How you decide to think about yourself is going to make all the difference in the person **you** will become.

The most important decisions in your life right now are entirely up to *you*. The first one we already talked about: deciding whether or not you will have a relationship with Jesus. And this decision is the second most important one: will you begin a relationship with yourself?

Sounds strange, I know. Here is what I mean: will you be your own best friend? Will you begin now, to tell yourself, the good news about yourself? You are amazing. You are incredible. You are normal. You are the best kind of friend. You are loved. You are accepted.

If you say, "Yes! I will be the best friend to me that I can be!" then it's time to get started. Start with telling yourself the truth about who you are, based on the verse you read earlier. If you're not quite ready to take this step, hang in there, friend. Keep pouring God's truth into your heart.

"You're beautiful from head to toe, my dear love, beautiful beyond compare, absolutely flawless." Song of Solomon 4:7 (MSG) Go ahead—read it out loud so that gorgeous heart of yours can hear it.

You are beautiful. You are absolutely flawless.

So that pimple on your face? That's no flaw! That is simply your body's beauty spot. And you are on your way to becoming a beautiful woman from a beautiful girl!

BECOMING BRAVE

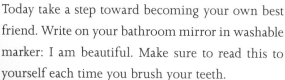

Today take a step toward becoming your own best friend. Write on your bathroom mirror in washable marker: I am beautiful. Make sure to read this to yourself each time you brush your teeth.

COURAGEOUS CALL

Dear Jesus, I need You. Help me to see myself as You see me. When negative thoughts try to set up a home inside my head, please help me to kick them out. You say that I am absolutely flawless and I am going to believe You! In Jesus' name, Amen.

CHAPTER 16

I AM HIS

mean girls, loved, self-worth, friends,
hurt, beauty, body changes

Coming back from lunch break, you sit down at your desk, holding back the well of tears threatening to spill from your eyes.

Why would she say that about me? you can't help but wonder. You keep thinking back over the conversation you heard between the girls at the table next to yours. Their conversation was about you and it hurt. You've never been mean to either one of them, so why would they say mean things about you?

As girls are growing up, sometimes I think there is some confusion. We think that if we can make another person look bad, it makes us look good. This is definitely a little messed up.

Since we can't control what someone else says, how can we guard our hearts when someone's comments make us feel ugly?

Feeling unaccepted is nothing new. If you read through the Bible, you'll find lots of people who at one point or another felt unloved or rejected. Even Jesus was "looked down on and passed over" Isaiah 53:3 (MSG)

Remembering who we are in God's eyes helps to heal the hurt that comes from meanness. When I know that the Lord accepts me, it puts me exactly where I need to be to deal with ugly words. Yet, when my heart is hurting from words that have been said by others, it doesn't automatically go to the positive things God has said about me. Instead, I have to remind my heart of what God says.

He has filled the Bible with many verses about how He feels about you:

- "My beloved is mine and I am his." (Song of Solomon 2:16 NLT)
- "See what great love the Father has lavished on us, that we should be called children of God!" (1 John 3:1 NIV)
- "You are a chosen people, a royal priesthood, a holy nation, God's special possession." (1 Peter 2:9 NIV)

BECOMING BRAVE

When mean words come your way, chances are you are not going to be near your Bible or this book to help remind you of what God has said about you. That's why I put God's truth everywhere, where I can read it over and over again.

When we feel rejected, God's words remind us that we are accepted. But not just accepted—we are the "apple of His eye." (Zechariah 2:8)

Choose one of the verses listed above to memorize. I know memorizing can be hard. Start by reading the verse you choose three times a day: once before school, once after school, and just before you go to bed.

COURAGEOUS CALL

Thank you, Jesus, that You are mine and I am Yours. Heal my heart when others wound me with words. Help me to respond in a way that would honor You and the person You have created me to be. In Jesus' name, Amen.

CHAPTER 17

I WON'T FORGET YOU

God's love, feeling loved

Have you ever forgotten something? Something really important?

Maybe you were given the responsibility of feeding your dog, but you forgot. Your poor dog had to go all day without eating and you felt terrible. When I was younger, I would often forget to do the chores my mom asked me to do. (Or was that really me just putting it off until I forgot on purpose?)

Well, I probably shouldn't admit this, but one day, I was at home working away, when suddenly I remembered. *I forgot to get Madi from school!* The pick-up time had come and gone and I completely missed getting my own daughter from school.

When I finally arrived, Madi was a ball of emotions: mad, sad, and everything in between. She had a right to be. Who in the world would forget their own child?

Not only have I been the one who has forgotten someone, but sometimes I feel forgotten. I have felt forgotten when I haven't been invited to something fun my friends are doing. I have had birthdays when none of my friends remembered.

I have even felt like God has forgotten me. Today, I became really frustrated when something I was trying to do didn't work. I asked God, "Where are you? Why aren't you helping me?"

Have you ever felt that way?

You have? I thought so. You, too, know what it is like to feel like you haven't been remembered; left behind and left out.

I can tell you who will never forget you. God!

Isaiah 49:15 (NLT) says, "Never! Can a mother forget her nursing child? Can she feel no love for the child she has borne? But even if that were possible, I would not forget you!"

God says it is absolutely impossible for Him to forget you. He could never do it!

One thing makes my heart feel better when I feel forgotten: remembering what God says. He will not and cannot forget about me. He always holds me close to his heart. Even today, while I **felt** frustrated, He was with me.

GETTING TO KNOW YOU

(Circle one answer below each question.)

What is your favorite way to be remembered on your birthday?

a. A special wake-up breakfast.

b. Getting to choose your favorite activity for the day.

c. Picking out a place to go to dinner.

What is the best way for someone to let you know they're thinking of you?

a. A special note.

b. Saying, "You're special to me."

c. A little gift.

What is your favorite way to let someone else know you remember him or her?

a. Draw them a picture.

b. Give them a huge hug; telling them you love them.

c. Buying them something they like.

COURAGEOUS CALL

Dear Jesus, thank you for never forgetting about me. Please help me remember when I feel forgotten by others, You are thinking of me. In Jesus' name, Amen.

CHAPTER 18

RIGHT THROUGH IT ALL

God's love, feeling loved

When I was younger I really didn't mind being sick. Sick meant I got to stay home from school with Mom. She would make me comfy on the couch, turning the TV on to my favorite show. All day long, she would bring me drinks and food to help me feel better. When I was sick, I knew that I was loved.

I think Jesus and my mom thought alike. In Matthew 14, we read a story about Jesus meeting a lot of sick people. He, Himself, was feeling very sad. His cousin, John the Baptist had just died. He wanted to be alone, but when His boat landed, there were many people, thousands of people, waiting for Him. They had heard He could heal their illnesses. Instead of wishing they would go away, verse 14 tells us, ". . . he had compassion on them and healed their sick." (NIV) He showed His love for them by caring for them.

After He healed them, they didn't go away. In fact, the crowd stayed, even as it began to become nighttime. His disciples told

Jesus, "Send these people away so they can go and buy food for themselves." Jesus didn't want them to be sent away. He loved them. Instead, He told the disciples to figure out a way to feed them; all 5,000 of them! All they found were five loaves and two fish. Jesus took what they had and miraculously fed everyone.

Just as Jesus loved and cared for the people when they were sick and hungry, Jesus cares for you even when you are not at your best. His love for us doesn't depend on whether or not we are having a great day or our worst. He just loves us through it all.

You may get the feeling that in order to be loved, you have to be perfect. Get straight As in school. Sit in the best seat in band. Take first place in the race and win every game. Get invited to the popular parties and be in the "in" crowd. That might be the message others are sending, but that is never the heart of Jesus. His words to you are words of love, no matter how you are feeling or what you are doing.

The more we tell our heart these words of truth, the more fearless we become. We begin to fear less. Knowing we are loved perfectly and unconditionally by Jesus, makes us brave, even if we **never** have one A on a report card or get invited to the party.

BECOMING BRAVE

I talked about how my mom took care of me when I was sick. What types of things make you feel loved?

COURAGEOUS CALL

Dear Jesus, stories in the Bible that show how You loved others help me to know how You love me. Thank you for coming to earth to show us just how much we are loved and how to love other people. In Jesus' name, Amen.

I'm Loved

CHAPTER 19

YOU DON'T HAVE TO CHANGE A THING

God's love, self-worth, self-esteem, value, body

Most of us can think of something about ourselves that we'd like to change or something other people have told us we need to change.

For me at your age, it was being what my teachers called "too loud."

Every report card I received informed my parents that I talked too much in class. I would always promise my mom I would do better and I meant to. Really, I did. Once I got in class though . . . it just seemed impossible. There were so many hours to be quiet and not enough minutes to chat. For all my talking, there were consequences that followed.

The worst consequence came in sixth grade. My teacher decided the only way to keep me quiet was to put my desk right next to his. Not in front or behind his, but right next to it. Close

75

enough that he could reach out and touch my arm if I started talking.

So embarrassing!

"Too loud" became the label I wore.

I am sure my teacher didn't mean to make me feel like I was flawed, but that is how I felt.

Until I started discovering God's words about me.

In Zechariah 2:8 (NIV) God tells how he feels about those he loves, ". . . for whoever touches you touches the apple of his eye."

We are the apples of his eye. We are a sweet spot in His heart.

Reading those words began to change the way I saw myself. Yes, I did need to learn self-control. But God didn't see me like my teachers saw me—He said I was sweet to Him.

Knowing someone thought of me and loved me like that, made it a whole lot easier for me to love myself. I realized God knew exactly what He was doing when He made me to be a girl who loves words. Now, I need a lot of them!

Is there something about you that someone has said you need to change? How does that make you feel? Changing is not a bad thing; in fact, it can be very good. Every day I hope that I am changing, growing into a person who is more and more like Jesus. But I also am embracing that even if I never change, God still thinks I'm sweet to Him.

BECOMING BRAVE

Whenever you see an apple, remind yourself: I am the apple of God's eye.

COURAGEOUS CALL

Dear God, help me to bravely face the changes I need to make in order to become more mature. Help me remember that me changing and You loving me have nothing to do with each other. You say I am the apple of your eye! In Jesus' name, Amen.

I'm Loved

CHAPTER 20

EYES ON YOU

God's love, scared, love, care

When my daughters played softball, as they walked up to the plate to bat, their coach would call out "Keep your eye on the ball!" Their coach knew that if their eyes were on the ball, when it came sailing across that plate, their bat would connect with it. The bat wasn't their focus nor the outfield where they wanted their ball to go. Their eyes were on the most important thing: the ball.

God tells us, because of His great love, He's got his loving eyes on us. "But the eyes of the LORD are on those who fear him, on those whose hope is in his unfailing love." Psalm 33:18 (NIV)

God goes on in the next verse to explain that He keeps His eyes on us because He is protecting us from harm.

Jesus is looking at you today. He is fully aware of everything that is going on in your life; the fun stuff and the not-so-fun stuff. He also loves watching you enjoy life. He sees you feeling alone at times; even invisible. He knows you want so much to live for Him and He knows you struggle at times to do what is right.

No matter what happens today, even if you completely mess up and make everyone angry and upset, His eyes are still on you. Not eyes of anger if you do it wrong. Not eyes rolling, thinking, *She did it again?!* His eyes are eyes of love. He wants to help you. He wants to protect you as you keep Your eyes on Him each and every day.

BECOMING BRAVE

What is one thing happening in your life right now that you find comfort in knowing God has His eyes on you? Share below. Then, look in the mirror at your eyes and say to yourself: The eyes of the Lord are on me.

_____

_____

_____

_____

COURAGEOUS CALL

Dear Jesus, thank you for having Your eyes on me. I know I'm not a little child anymore; I don't need someone watching my every move. But it is good to know that someone, One as powerful as You, is watching over me and every move I make. In Jesus' name, Amen.

CHAPTER 21

GOOD WORK!

purpose, value, self-worth

Last year, I had the opportunity to travel to the other side of the world, to India. My friends and I got to see some of the good work God is doing there. He is using His people to teach those who have never had the opportunity to learn to read, do math, or learn how to take care of their families. The best part of all is that these beautiful people are learning about Jesus for the very first time! When I arrived home from India, I knew God wanted me to tell everyone about Mission India and encourage others to help too.

Not everyone is able to travel around the world to help others, but everyone has good work to do. My niece, Carley, shared with me that last summer she went to Vacation Bible School. The church was preparing for a mission trip to Haiti, so they were collecting sunglasses, beach balls, and money. Carley sent in a pair of sunglasses, a beach ball, and a dollar. She said, "Even though that's not much, all that the people in Haiti have for a playground is cement ground with brick walls around it. No basketballs or hoops, no monkey bars, or slides."

When God saw what Carley chose to do for the people of Haiti, I'm sure He said, "Good work!" Carley is doing exactly what He created her to do. Ephesians 2:10 (NLT) tells us, "For we are God's masterpiece. He has created us anew in Christ Jesus, so we can do the good things he planned for us long ago."

Look at all that goodness rolled into one verse. You and I are God's masterpiece—His greatest work of art. He created us to do good things. Each time we do well, we're doing exactly what He created us to do.

There are opportunities for you to do good all around you, every day. It is not easy to do good work. In fact, it is so much easier to choose to do what is easy or selfish; at least it is for me. Yet, God made you and me to do this good work and I have found that when I do, I have so much fun!

Look for a way that you can do good work today. Look for someone you can help or something you can do to make the world a better place. Come back here and write out what you did afterward.

GETTING TO KNOW YOU

(Circle one answer below each question.)

What are your favorite ways to help?

a. Taking care of babies or toddlers.

b. Doing work for others.

c. Helping elderly adults with physical tasks.

When it comes to working, what type of work do you like best?

a. Physical work; working with my hands.

b. Mental work; working with my mind.

c. Both; working with my hands and mind together.

How do you feel about volunteering?

a. I get excited any time I can help.

b. I haven't had an opportunity to give it a try.

c. It doesn't seem fun to me.

COURAGEOUS CALL

Dear Jesus, I am excited to learn about the good work You have given me to do. Help me see how I can help others. Help me to be brave enough to do it! In Jesus' name, Amen.

CHAPTER 22

YOU'RE NOT OUT OF YOUR MIND

purpose, value, self-worth

Every one of us has a purpose and that purpose is to make God famous. We are to help others know Him and discover the love He has for them. For each of us, the way that we do that looks a bit different.

There is a girl in the Bible whose story is told in Acts 12. Rhoda was her name and she was a servant in the house of a woman named Mary. Peter, one of Jesus' disciples and the leader of the Christians, had been thrown in prison for sharing about Jesus. They put Peter in prison while he waited to go through a trial. It seems the government was going to kill him for his boldness for Jesus.

The night before Peter's trial, Christians gathered together at Mary's house and prayed all night long for him.

Peter was sleeping, chained between two soldiers. An angel came, removed his chains, and helped him escape! Peter went to Mary's home and began knocking on the entrance. Rhoda ran toward the door and when she heard Peter calling out, she ran back to the others exclaiming, "Peter is at the door!"

"You're out of your mind," they told her. When she kept insisting that it was so, they said, "It must be his angel." Acts 12:15 (NIV) Rhoda wouldn't give up. She kept insisting that they pay attention to her until finally they went to the door to see that it was, in fact, Peter.

Rhoda had a job. Even though it was the middle of the night and her tasks were most likely done for the day, she still did her job. She had a big part in Peter being delivered safely back to his people from prison.

Even though the adults made fun of her, Rhoda didn't let them put her down. Bravely, she insisted she knew what she was talking about. She didn't give up until they went to see for themselves.

There may be times when you feel others will not listen to you because you are young. They may think you don't know what is best or right. Like Rhoda, be brave. Hang in there and persevere.

Rhoda was rewarded when the adults got to the gate and discovered it was in fact Peter. Peter encouraged them and they all benefitted from Rhoda being brave.

BECOMING BRAVE

Have you experienced a time when an adult wouldn't listen to you and you really needed them to? How did it turn out?

_____

_____

_____

COURAGEOUS CALL

Dear Jesus, just because I am young, it doesn't mean You won't use me now. Like Rhoda, give me a job to do and then help me be brave to do it. In Jesus' name, Amen.

My Purpose

CHAPTER 23

HIS IDEAS

purpose, good works, value, self-worth

Have you ever prepared a surprise for someone you loved? I think planning surprises for others is even more fun than being surprised myself (and I love surprises).

I knew my daughter, Madi, would love the surprise I planned for her birthday. Her favorite band was in America—all the way from England. Knowing it might possibly be a once-in-a-lifetime opportunity; I purchased our family tickets to the concert as a gift.

It was all I could do to keep it a secret. In fact, there were many times I almost slipped. I finally did tell her sister and then made her promise not to tell.

Madi's birthday finally came. When she opened her gift, she screamed! She was completely shocked. I know that she was excited to get that gift, but I think I was just as excited giving it to her.

Those concert tickets were nothing compared to what God says He has planned for you.

In the Bible it says, "No eye has seen, no ear has heard, and no mind has imagined what God has prepared for those who love him." 1 Corinthians 2:9 (NLT)

Read that verse again; it's a lot to take in. God, the creator of everything, has a plan for you because He loves you. He is in the process of bringing that plan all together. What He has planned for us is beyond anything we could come up with!

What is the greatest idea you can think of for your life?

This verse tells us God's plan is even better than that! It's unlike anything we have ever heard of or imagined. He has planned it all for those who love Him. That's me. And that's you.

Our lives are like puzzle pieces. And at just the right time, God will add pieces to create the whole picture. How exciting! We don't have anything to fear because God has the plan all down.

Our part is to just keep loving, learning about, and obeying Him and saying "yes" to bravely walking with Him.

BECOMING BRAVE

God tells us we can fearlessly trust Him with our lives. How do you feel knowing that God has a plan for your life?

_____

_____

_____

_____

COURAGEOUS CALL

Dear Jesus, I can't wait to see all of the amazing things You have prepared for me. Help me stay close to You so that You can bring all the puzzle pieces together for my life. In Jesus' name, Amen.

CHAPTER 24

SET APART

purpose, good works, value, self-worth

When the children's choir from Africa came to sing at her school, Crissy knew—one day she was going to grow up to run an orphanage in Africa. She felt it strongly in her heart; God was going to use her as a missionary to orphans.

You may or may not have had an experience similar to Crissy's, but here is something I want you to know: God has a plan for you to partner with Him to share His love with others. He says to those of us who love Him: "Before I formed you in the womb I knew you, before you were born I set you apart . . ." Jeremiah 1:5 (NIV)

I wasn't quite sure what "set apart" really meant so I looked it up. Dictionary.com says "set" means . . . to put (something or someone) in a particular place. The word "apart" means: to or at one side. Let's put those two together: to put someone in a particular place or at one side.

That is what God does with us; when we are ready He puts us in a particular place so we show His love to others.

There can be many ways for Him to do that. He may make you sensitive to the girl walking alone in the halls or by herself at lunch. He might nudge you to invite some of your friends to go to church with you. He could wake you up in the middle of the night because someone needs you to pray for them. Often set apart means not doing things that you feel pressured to do like use apps your parents don't approve of or begging your parents for certain clothes so that you can be like everyone else.

Sometimes instead of feeling set apart or "set at one side," we can feel more like we are set aside. Shut out or left out.

Others might leave us out, but God never does. God draws us in. He pulls us close to include us in His plan to give us a life that honors Him and blesses us. The brave girl trusts that although she may at times feel shut out, God says she is set apart.

BECOMING BRAVE

What is an area in your life where you are struggling to be set apart? Do you feel pressure to dress a certain way or own a certain phone so that you are not "set aside?" Below, write in pencil any ways you feel like you have to do what others do so that you are not "set aside." Then as you pray today's Courageous Call, use your eraser to rub out these pressures, trusting God to take care of them for you.

_____

_____

_____

_____

COURAGEOUS CALL

Dear Lord, You say that I am set apart, not shut out. When I feel like I am excluded, help me to remember that I am absolutely included in Your good plans for me. In Jesus' name, Amen.

CHAPTER 25

NOT ALONE

rejection, hurt, friendships, growing up

Friendships were so different when Jayla and her big group of friends began texting. Being able to communicate whenever they wanted was the best! Some days, though, it was the worst.

Before they started texting, if just a couple of girls from their group got together it was ok. (Most moms wouldn't let all ten girls have a sleep over all together anyway.) Now that they could share pictures when just a few of them hung out, it was different. Knowing that you were the one not invited hurt; being excluded made Jayla feel sad. Jealous feelings and rejection took over. And Jayla found she felt a lot braver saying mean things on her iPod than she did in person.

This bravery wasn't the good kind and Jayla knew that. As she cried, she shared her unhappy feelings with her mom. This part of growing up wasn't fun. Her mom told her it just wasn't possible for the group to always be together. Friends should learn to be happy for each other instead of hurt each other. This happiness comes from loving each other and loving each other first comes from knowing how much God loves you. We don't have to let feelings of rejection and jealousy take over our hearts. Jayla is still not feeling happy about these feelings, but she is trying to understand.

God's Word tells us, "No, in all these things we are more than conquerors through him who loved us. For I am convinced that neither death nor life, neither angels nor demons, neither the present nor the future, nor any powers, neither height nor depth, nor anything else in all creation, will be able to separate us from the love of God that is in Christ Jesus our Lord." Romans 8:37–39 (NIV) As Jayla learns how very much God loves her, loving others will become easier for her.

GETTING TO KNOW YOU

(Circle one answer below each question.)

When I feel sad, I want to:

a. Be around my family.

b. Spend time with my friends.

c. Be alone.

When I need to be comforted, I prefer:

a. A hug.

b. Words of encouragement.

c. Hugs and words.

I feel comfortable crying:

a. Only at home.

b. Only in my room.

c. Wherever I'm feeling sad.

COURAGEOUS CALL

Dear Jesus, thank you for comforting me with Your love when I feel sad. Help me to be the brave one and love others, even when I am feeling unloved. In Jesus' name, Amen.

I'm Comforted

CHAPTER 26

HE FEELS TOO

sad, friendship, emotions, comfort

We sat on the floor in the empty house. Why did we have to go? We loved our church, our house, our town. Just two days ago, the now empty house had been filled with Christmas: people, laughter, and tasty treats. Now it was empty.

As we sat on the floor and cried, my family knew it was time to begin our move. The big moving truck taking our belongings a thousand miles away was pulling out of the driveway. Our broken hearts and bloodshot eyes wouldn't change the fact that we had to go.

Tears. They come from friendships that hurt, plans that get broken, and disappointment when things don't go the way we think they should.

Jesus knew tears too.

In John 11:35 Jesus' dear friend Lazarus dies, and his heart crumbled.

Maybe it's a little weird to think this way, but I'm glad Jesus felt sad. I'm glad because knowing that Jesus felt sadness when He was here on earth makes me feel less alone when I'm sad. Knowing He felt the same pain I feel helps me know He understands me.

You'll feel sad sometime in the future. You may be at school—where someone spoke words that hurt your heart. You could be on a ball field—walking away from striking out again. You might be in your room, looking at the social media picture you were not included in. Just as sadness was a normal part of Jesus' life, sadness will be a part of yours.

When those tears well up and fall down your cheeks, allow yourself the time you need. It might help you to find an adult or friend you can share your feelings with.

Other days, the best thing you can do is simply shut your eyes. Picture yourself crawling up in Jesus' lap. He's stroking your hair and whispering in your ear, "I've been there. Just let me hold you." You'll be amazed at the comfort this will bring.

Going to Jesus doesn't mean we're weak; in fact, it means we are brave. We are brave enough to admit we need Him. When we do, we'll find the comfort we need.

BECOMING BRAVE

What jobs do some people do that involve comforting people?

Do you know someone who is a nurse or a doctor? Interview them, asking them how giving comfort is a part of their work.

COURAGEOUS CALL

Dear Jesus, I am sorry that you experienced loss when you were here, but I am glad that even in sorrow, you understand me. In Jesus' name, Amen.

I'm Comforted

CHAPTER 27

REVEALING

growing, sad, hurt

Have you ever felt sad but didn't really know why?

Yesterday, my friend asked me several times through the day, "What's wrong?" My answer: "I don't know." Sincerely, I didn't. I knew that I felt tired, but outside of that, I wasn't sure what was going on with me.

One of the things that makes me happy to be in a relationship with Jesus is that even when I don't know what is going on with my feelings, He does. He can help.

Jesus can reveal to us exactly what we need even before we know that we need it.

My problem yesterday was that I was tired. I had stayed up way too late, getting pulled into a really good book I was reading. While the reading was great, being tired the next day wasn't. Sometimes when I am tired, it is harder for me to be nice. When I am not nice I feel guilty.

Jesus tells us in 1 John 3:20 (NLT), "Even if we feel guilty, God is greater than our feelings, and he knows everything."

God is greater than my feelings. He can forgive me when I do wrong and then help me move past negative feelings that try to control my day. I don't have to be fearful of the feelings controlling me; they don't have to. I can find courage to control my feelings.

You know those days when you really don't know what is going on inside your head and heart? Meanness seems to be festering inside? A rude comment at school keeps playing over and over again in your mind?

Jesus knows. He can and wants to help you know what's wrong too. He wants to identify the trouble in your heart. When you can see it for what it is, you can allow Him to help you. He'll heal the hurt so that you can be whole again.

Each one of us was created with a space—a space that only Jesus can fill. You may wish that you didn't have any problems, I do too, but God can use our problems. Our troubles can be the thing that causes us to turn to Jesus, and *that* is a very good thing.

BECOMING BRAVE

One thing that helps me understand myself is writing in a journal. Ask your mom to get you a plain, smooth-covered journal. Make the cover of the journal reflect you. You might doodle on it, cut out pictures and glue them on the cover, or find some of your favorite stickers. Use this journal as a safe place to write out all your feelings—happy, sad, and everything in between.

COURAGEOUS CALL

Dear Jesus, I don't like having problems. They can hurt.
Help me to allow my troubles to steer me closer to You!
In Jesus' name, Amen.

I'm Comforted

CHAPTER 28

HE IS WITHIN ME

growing, sad, hurt, heaven, family

When I was a young woman, my daddy passed away. I wasn't as young as you, but I was still too young to not have my daddy here on earth with me. I understood that he was now in heaven with God, but I missed him here with me.

One day when my dad was getting ready to die, I was staying with him at the hospital. It was my birthday and my heart was sad to know that I was saying good-bye to my dad. That day, God brought his comfort to me in a very kind way. When I was going home from the hospital, I heard a song on the radio that talked about being completely healed and the way that healing came was by going to heaven and getting a new body.

That day, I knew in a way I had never known before, that God was with me. Not only was He with me, but He was within me. He was comforting my heart in a way that didn't make sense. My daddy was dying, but my heart felt peaceful.

David writes these words of strength in Psalm 46:5 (NLT),

"God is within her, she will not fall; God will help her at break of day." When I left the hospital that day, it was morning. I had stayed all night long with my daddy. That was when God was showing me that He was within me.

David writes more beautiful verses leading up to this one: "God is our refuge and strength, an ever-present help in trouble. Therefore we will not fear, though the earth give way and the mountains fall into the heart of the sea, though its waters roar and foam and the mountains quake with their surging." Psalm 46:1–3 (NIV)

Just because you are young, doesn't mean you don't experience hard things in life. Parents divorce, loved ones die, moves take us from our friends, and people do hurtful things. Even while all these things are going on around you, God is within you. He is your refuge, strength, and help in trouble. He is empowering you to be brave. Because He is with us and within us, we will not fear . . . not anything. No matter what is coming together or falling apart, we can snuggle close to Him and receive the bravery we need to keep right on going.

BECOMING BRAVE

I want you to shut your eyes and imagine yourself in a storm. The storm is that hard thing you are going through right now. Now picture Jesus walking into that storm. He lifts you up and together you walk right out of it. That is what He is doing for you today!

COURAGEOUS CALL

Dear Jesus, thank you that in You I will not fall. You are within me and You are helping me today and every day. In Jesus' name, Amen.

CHAPTER 29

MIRROR, MIRROR, ON THE WALL

value, self-worth, self-esteem, beauty, body changes, be myself

Did you grow up watching fairy tale movies? It would be crazy to count how many times I have watched *Snow White and the Seven Dwarfs*. In Disney's early movies, so many of the heroines had blonde hair. I was glad to have at least one princess, Snow White, who looked a bit more like me.

One character in this movie really scared me—that nasty queen. She was so mean to Snow White, her cruel character only made Snow White all the more beautiful.

My heart goes out to the cold queen. I feel sorry for her. "Mirror, mirror on the wall, who is the fairest of them all?" she asks.

What kind of woman asks a mirror what it thinks in order to feel better about herself?

I am sorry to say I have. I've definitely looked in the mirror, hoping to see something that would make me feel good about myself. A good hair day, perhaps? That blemish on my forehead smaller than the day before?

As I grow closer and closer to Jesus, I have learned the very best place to go when I need to know that I am beautiful. Jesus' love letter to me—the Bible.

"You are priceless to me. I love you and honor you. So I will trade other people for you. I will give up other nations to save your lives." Isaiah 43:4 (NIrV) He goes on to say, "I created them to bring glory to me. I formed them and made them." Isaiah 43:7b

When I look in the mirror each morning, I am really looking at a choice. I can choose to criticize the image that I see. Finding fault is oh-so-easy! Picking at the picture I see, it's just too simple to pull that girl apart.

I can also choose to be courageous. I can fearlessly leave the fault-finding to those on Facebook, TV commercials, or ads in the mall. I can confidently know that I don't need to copy someone else's look. I can confidently be me.

The One whose opinion matters most says I am priceless to Him. He says He loves you and me; He formed us and made us to be exactly as we are. He tells us we are created for one thing: to bring Him glory.

Like the mirror reflects your image back to you, you were created to reflect God's beauty back to Him. Not just to God alone, but you were also made to bring God's beauty to those around you. That beauty looks like: love, joy, peace, patience, kindness, goodness, gentleness, and self-control. It's a beauty much more permanent than a good hair day!

GETTING TO KNOW YOU

(Circle one answer below each question.)

How many times a day do you look in the mirror?

a. 10 (morning, night, and every time I go in the bathroom).

b. 15 (same as above, plus a few times in between).

c. 25 (I am so scared something will be wrong and I won't know).

The modern mirror, like we have in our homes, was invented in 1835. How do you feel about this invention?

a. This was a great invention.

b. I wish it had never been invented.

c. It doesn't really matter to me.

How do you usually feel when you look in the mirror?

a. It makes me feel good.

b. It makes me feel bad.

c. Neither, I just use it to make sure I don't have a boogie in my nose.

COURAGEOUS CALL

Dear Lord, thank you for making me. Thank you for my eyes, my nose, and my chin. Thank you that in You I can fear less and not find fault with the me I see in the mirror. I can, instead, see the girl You are growing me to be. In Jesus' name, Amen.

CHAPTER 30

GORGEOUS JAR

growing self-worth, value, beauty, being me

Some of my daughter's favorite things are her plants. She likes to make her orchid, bonsai, and succulents at home all around my kitchen sink, right by the big, backyard-looking window. (If you've never heard of these plants, ask a parent to show them to you at a nursery. Take a look at my scrapbook on my website at LynnCowell.com to see Madi's plants around my window. Just click on the "Books" tab.)

Each one of Madi's four plants is set in a clay pot. Day in and day out, each pot does its job really well. You could say that Madi depends on them; but really, she never thinks about the pots, even the bonsai's, which is a beautiful, blue-glazed one.

Why doesn't Madi wash, shine, or care for the pots? She never draws attention to them or wishes for one that is fancier.

Why not?

The pots are not what really matter. What is really important is what is **inside** the pot. God didn't create plants to make pots look good; pots are made to show off the prized plants. The jar's job is simply to display the beauty and uniqueness of God's creation. The bright hue of the purple orchid. The unique shape of the clipped bonsai. The strength of the succulent. The plant, what is in the pot, is the treasure, so that is where Madi focuses her attention.

2 Corinthians 4:7 (NIV) says, "But we have this treasure in jars of clay to show that this all-surpassing power is from God and not from us."

This verse tells us that what is important is what is in the jars (and we are the jars), Christ who lives in us. He is our beauty. He is our confidence.

So how, like this verse says, do we show His "all-surpassing power"? We show His power best when we are in situations where we naturally don't have what it takes. When we are in over our heads. That's when we can show off His power. We have to get His help to do what we need to do. Then we can tell others how He helped us.

So often we spend our energy, time, and emotions focusing on our "jar:" our grades, clothes, or the fun this weekend.

When you and I focus our energy, time, and emotions nurturing the treasure of His life in us, we grow like the plants. We choose not to build our security and self-worth on what's on the outside like the grades, the clothes, and the fun because these are all things we can lose or have taken from us. Instead, we grow in strength, beauty, and in God's confidence. We can keep growing no matter what is going on around us.

When our attention is on what is **in** our jar rather than **on** our jar, that's when others will see Jesus' beauty in us.

BECOMING BRAVE

Growing plants can be fun! Let's grow our own.

You'll need to get:

- a pot (Choose a pot that is not fancy, purposefully plain.)
- potting soil
- seeds or a plant

Fill your pot with soil and plant your seeds or plant according to the instructions. Be sure to keep your plant in a spot where it gets the right amount of sun. Write out 2 Corinthians 4:7 on a pretty notecard, keeping it close to the pot as a reminder to focus on what is "inside" rather than what is "outside."

As you water your plant and make sure it gets the sunlight it needs, let it be a reminder to you to be intentional about taking care of the girl God is growing inside of you.

COURAGEOUS CALL

Dear Lord, when I look at plants, help me to think of how I am growing. The important part of me is what is on the inside. That is what I want to focus my attention on. In Jesus' name, Amen.

I'm Beautiful

CHAPTER 31

SHE JUST DIDN'T KNOW

value, self-worth, self-esteem, beauty, body changes

In John 4, Jesus stops beside a well to get a drink of water. There He meets a woman and strikes up a conversation. The woman is completely shocked that Jesus would talk to her! Just like in our world today, some people in Jesus' time believed they were better than other people. Jesus' family was Jewish and most Jewish people thought they were better than the family the woman at the well was from, who were Samaritans.

What she didn't know was Jesus is not like everyone else.

Jesus begins to explain to her that the thing she wants so much in life, to be loved, accepted, and to know she is beautiful, He can give Her. He goes on to say He can tell that she *doesn't* know how prized she is. How could Jesus know this about a complete stranger? First, because Jesus is God and He knows everything.

Second, Jesus can see, because of the way she is living, that she couldn't see her value. The woman had five husbands in her past and has another man in her life who isn't her husband yet.

Friend, when you know that you are worth everything to Jesus and loved beyond anything in the world, your actions show that. The way you dress, take care of your body, and talk about yourself, all reveal whether or not you understand how much you are loved.

Sometimes as girls get older, we begin feeling comfortable voicing negative things about ourselves. It might be a way to get others to give you compliments as they disagree with your harsh talk. It could also be that you really believe it.

Either way, a brave beauty doesn't have to go there when other girls do. She knows she is beautifully and wonderfully made by the Creator of all, and she knows He only makes what is beautiful.

BECOMING BRAVE

I am not saying you should ignore the things about yourself that you don't like. But what if you began to realize the things you don't like are actually gifts from God? When I was in high school, I was very flat chested. (Actually that never changed!) I was very self-conscious about it, especially when others made fun of me. But you know what? When I ran, I was very glad! That part of my body was perfect for the runner in me and I began to be thankful. If you have a part of yourself that you struggle to see as beautiful, what can you do to see it differently?

_____

_____

_____

_____

COURAGEOUS CALL

Thank you, Jesus, for making me beautiful. Help me see what You see, Lord, and help me to never forget it! In Jesus' name, Amen.

CHAPTER 32

MASTERPIECE

value, self-worth, self-esteem, beauty, body changes

In my office, I have a book that I have had for a very long time. Filled with pages and pages of art, it highlights the best work of many well-known artists. I took it down just a few minutes ago to enjoy the incredible work created by talented artists, many of them hundreds of years ago. These beautiful pieces of work are highlighted in this book because they are the best of the best—masterpieces.

As I carefully looked at each one, I had a hard time imagining the kind of talent these artists had. I may not have the skills of an artist, but I know someone else who does. Jesus.

Dictionary.com says masterpiece means: a person's greatest piece of work, done with masterly skill.

Ephesians 2:10 (ESV) says "For we are God's masterpiece. He has created us anew in Christ Jesus, so we can do the good things he planned for us long ago."

Insert your name here along with the definition of masterpiece into this verse.

"_____ is part of God's greatest piece of work, one that God made with masterly skills."

Wow! That's a lot to take in. You are God's greatest work, His masterpiece. He created us so wonderfully so that we can do the good things He planned for us a long time ago.

Is that what you think when you look in the mirror? I am God's masterpiece.

You are! If that is not what you see, you've got some work to do, friend. We need to believe and see what God sees in us.

BECOMING BRAVE

Look in a book or online at artwork created by master artists like Van Gogh, Monet, and da Vinci. Each one of these works of art is beautiful because of the details that make up the masterpiece. What details do you see in yourself that make up the masterpiece God created you to be?

_____

_____

_____

_____

COURAGEOUS CALL

Dear Jesus, open my eyes to see myself as You do. I am beautiful. I am a masterpiece. In Jesus' name, Amen.

CHAPTER 33

MORE THAN SKIN DEEP

values, self-worth, self-esteem, beauty, body changes

As soon as Allie's body started changing, so did her skin. It didn't matter what she tried, nothing would make her acne go away.

Allie made a choice though. She chose to not let her acne slow her down, stop her, or cause her not to smile. She came to realize early on that it's not the condition of her skin that matters, it's the condition of her heart. Her heart for Jesus and others is what makes her beautiful.

The last time she and her mom went to visit her skin doctor, he asked her, "Does your acne cause you to be depressed? Does it affect your self-worth or your quality of life?"

Allie looked at him funny. She was shocked and surprised by his question. She boldly told the doctor that not only does she love who God made her to be, but she has tons of family and friends who care nothing about her acne. Why should she?

Of course Allie wouldn't mind not having acne, but Allie's

confidence comes from God, not makeup or clear skin. As a swimmer, she doesn't wear makeup to cover her blemishes. She is unafraid to show who she really is; allowing her inner beauty to be radiant. She understands the power behind 1 Peter 3:3–6 (NIV), "Your beauty should not come from outward adornment, such as elaborate hairstyles and the wearing of gold jewelry or fine clothes. Rather, it should be that of your inner self, the unfading beauty of a gentle and quiet spirit, which is of great worth in God's sight. For this is the way the holy women of the past who put their hope in God used to adorn themselves. They submitted themselves to their own husbands, like Sarah, who obeyed Abraham and called him her lord. You are her daughters if you do what is right and *do not give way to fear.*"

When it comes to her skin and how she looks, Allie does not give way to fear or let it hold her back.

Now, Allie leads worship for youth group and during Sunday services at church. This year she also has stepped up to leading a Bible study at her public high school without shrinking back.

I'm not saying that if we struggle with our appearance we are not strong. This is one of those battles some of us have to work through our whole lives; to not base our value on our appearance. Here is what I am learning though—when a girl has God's power in her, she can learn to become fearless, beautiful, and brave—no matter what the world says is "beautiful".

BECOMING BRAVE

Sometimes lots of beauty talk can stress a girl out! Let's relax in who God says we are by making some Stress-Less Bath Salts. Salt on your skin can improve relaxation.

Here's what you'll need:

- 2 cups Epsom salts or magnesium flakes
- 1/2 cup baking soda
- 1/4 cup sea salt (optional)

Choice one of the essential oils combinations below:

- 30 drops of lavender essential oils + 10 drops of peppermint essential oil
- 10 drops spearmint oil + 5 drops rosemary oil
- 5 drops eucalyptus oil + 15 drops lavender oil (this is good for sore muscles)

1. Mix all ingredients together.
2. Store in a zip-sealed bag or air-tight jar. Use 1/4 cup at a time.

SECTION 2

I AM BRAVE

I Can Be Me

CHAPTER 34

WHO DO I WANT TO BE?

bravery, courage, self-confidence, fear, be yourself

Remember the diary I found from my tween years? Read some of my swirling thoughts in sixth grade (note the dates after each entry):

". . . Right now I don't think much about boys. I may act like it, but I don't."—March 23

"Sam called and asked me to "go" with him. I didn't want to, but my best friend told him I said 'yes'."—March 26

"Today, nothing much happened. I don't know how my friend got me in this mess with Sam and I don't know what to do. Lord, get me out!"—March 27

"I broke up with Sam. Boy, am I glad I did. But he asked me to go out with him again. Ugh!"—March 28

What a struggle! It doesn't even matter that my trouble was

with a boy. There were many other times I wrote about frustrated feelings with friends and family and confusion on what do to.

Do you know what the problem was with many of my problems?

I was fearful of people. I wasn't sure of the girl I was or the girl I wanted to be. So I often found myself acting all sorts of ways, so I could be the person I thought my friends and family wanted.

Like the situation with Sam.

God has since shown me in His Word that I don't have to spin like the Tilt-O-Whirl at the amusement park; trying to be everything to everybody. As I am maturing and becoming the one He created me to be, I don't have to get on that ride. I'm becoming more and more brave every day.

Ephesians 4:14 (NLT) tells us: "Then we will no longer be immature like children. We won't be tossed and blown about by every wind of new teaching. We will not be influenced when people try to trick us with lies so clever they sound like the truth." Paul is telling us we don't have to believe all the things people say about God; that can make us shaky. We need to believe what God says about Himself.

The same is true when we spin this way and that, believing things that are not true about ourselves and then trying to be someone we are not. It makes us shaky inside—insecure. In this time of growing from child to adult, God can help you so your life doesn't feel like you're constantly pushed one way and then the other. He can make you brave and give you courage to be the true you.

GETTING TO KNOW YOU

(Circle an answer below each question.)

When your friend wants to do something you don't want to do, do you usually:

a. Go along with it.
b. Speak up and say what you want to do.
c. It depends on the situation.

How often do you feel afraid of what others will think of you?

a. All of the time.
b. Some of the time.
c. Never.

How often do the decisions you make have to do with the decisions your friends are making?

a. All the time; I want to do the same things they do.
b. Some of the time; it all depends on what the decision is.
c. Never; I decide to do what I want to do and if my friends do it too, great.

COURAGEOUS CALL

Dear Jesus, I don't want to do what I think is right, I want to do what You say is right. Help me learn to be brave and ask You for wisdom instead of feeling like I'm constantly being pushed around. In Jesus' name, Amen.

I Can Be Me

CHAPTER 35

NEB THE NERVOUS

bravery, courage, self-confidence, fear

Daniel 3 tells one of my favorite stories. It is a tale of bravery. This story takes place in a city called Babylon, long before Jesus was born. You can find where Babylon used to be—just look on a world map for the country of Iraq.

King Nebuchadnezzar was Babylon's king. Isn't that an awful name? Let's call him Neb. King Neb had some huge issues.

Have you ever watched a sporting event where an athlete celebrates like crazy every time he does something right, like doing a dance after a touchdown? Neb thought he was even cooler than those guys!

King Neb thought he was so great, he made a gold statue of himself that was as tall as a nine story building! He set this statue in a big field and gathered all the pretty and popular people to show it to. He wanted to impress everyone and make them think he was amazing.

Why would King Neb make such a huge statue . . . of himself?

He was trying hard to be liked.

Maybe you've had some experiences with social media, where you've seen people setting up a snap, trying to create a perfect picture of who they want to be. When you look at the picture and you think of that girl you see at school each day . . . well, you realize they don't really match.

Last year, I followed a lady on social media. I really liked her style. Every day she would post a #OOTD—outfit of the day. Do you know, I had to stop following her? Not because of her, but because of me. I found myself wanting to be like her instead of wanting to just be me.

When I look at Neb and all he was doing, I think his and my struggle were the same thing. I think Neb wrestled with being himself. Fearful of what others thought of him, I think he doubted that he was great just the way he was. Neb needed people to like him. He was fearful instead of fearless.

If we are brave and believe God's word when He says we are amazing just the way we are, we don't have to prove it. We know deep inside that we are special. That's when we can fear less and leave being fearful behind.

BECOMING BRAVE

Have you ever done something to try to get others to like you? Why do you think you did that?

_____

_____

_____

_____

COURAGEOUS CALL

Dear Jesus, I just want to be me, but sometimes I'm afraid others won't like me just as I am. Help me to like myself and trust You to bring friends into my life who like me for myself too. In Jesus' name, Amen.

I Can Be Me

CHAPTER 36

A FULL HEART

bravery, courage, self-confidence, fear

Every year before school started, my friend Jane would get a new wardrobe in all the coolest styles.

Before we started fifth grade, Jane and I went to the mall together. Jane brought money to buy new clothes. I didn't. She got white jeans, which I wanted too. I didn't just want the same white jeans as Jane, I also wanted the same shoes, shirts, and whole style as Jane. I wanted to look like Jane. When I asked my mom for these things, she reminded me: You are not Jane. You are Lynn.

While my mom's advice was wise, I didn't want to listen. Instead, I chose a feel-sorry-for-myself session.

Maybe your struggle to just be yourself is in band, when you hear the first chair play the flute. *If only I could play like her!* you think. Or on the ball field, as you walk up to the plate, your mind says, *I wouldn't be so scared if I knew I could slug it like she does!*

When thoughts like these come to mind, all the power is yours. You can hop on that slide and land in sadness. But you could also take this great advice from Proverbs: "For the despondent, every day brings trouble; for the happy heart, life is a continual feast." Proverbs 15:15 (NLT) When you choose to be happy, to be amazing you, misery moves out.

You can make the brave choice to move to having a happy heart. We can talk to ourselves; encouraging ourselves to not let our feelings take over. Courage is not a feeling; it is a choice. When you look up the definition, courage is a noun: the strength to go forward even in the face of fear; withstanding danger or difficulty.

When we choose to be happy as we are, even when we feel afraid to do so, our hearts turn toward happiness. Your heart will begin to feel full from your "continual feast" as Proverbs 15:15 called it.

You know that after school stomach grumbling? You'll eat just about anything you're so hungry.

How about after a holiday dinner, when your stomach is so full? If your parent asked, "Want a hamburger?" you'd say, "No way!"

Our tummy and our heart can be alike. If you focus on another person and wanting what she has, whether it is her backpack, her brains, or her boyfriend, you'll feel gloomy. You'll feel empty inside your heart like your stomach feels hollow when you're hungry. That's that slippery slope to a pity party. But if you choose to have a happy heart, you can say good-bye to those feelings of emptiness. There is no room for it here!

BECOMING BRAVE

Sometimes feeling happy is hard. You might need some help from a parent, pastor, or teacher if your sadness just won't seem to go away. That's ok; that is what adults are for. Find one you can trust and share your struggle with them. I also discovered something I could do every day that has helped me. I started a gratitude journal. It is a place I record good things from my day. From the butterfly I found in my backyard to things so much bigger, recounting the good things in my life helps me be happy!

COURAGEOUS CALL

Dear Jesus, You made me different from others. I am not exactly the same as anyone else. Sometimes my heart wants to be unhappy because I want to be the exact same as someone else. I want the same hairstyle, clothes, and brand names. Help me to choose to be happy and brave; to be just me! In Jesus' name, Amen.

CHAPTER 37

FINDING ME

bravery, courage, self-confidence, fear

Is there a certain activity the cool kids at your school do?

At Alexandra's school, all the cool kids play sports. For girls, the sport to play was softball. Every year since first grade, Alexandra had her mom sign her up to play too. Only there was a problem. Alexandra wasn't really great at softball. She struggled with fear every time she got up to the plate. Things in the outfield weren't much better.

No matter how much her mom tried to encourage her to try another activity, Alexandra wouldn't. Her closest friends all played softball; she wanted to as well. Then, Alexandra's doctor discovered something going wrong with her back—she had scoliosis. That means that as Alexandra's back grew, it wasn't growing straight. It had a curve in it. Her curve became so big her doctor suggested she have surgery to put two metal rods in her back to help straighten it out.

Alexandra was very scared. The surgery sounded painful. On top of that, her doctor told her that after the surgery there would be some things she couldn't do well and some things she couldn't do at all. Softball was one of them.

The year Alexandra chose to have the surgery, she didn't go out for softball. Instead, she joined a singing club and tried acting too. I'm sure you can guess what happened. She loved singing and acting and she was very good at both!

Take a moment to look up 1 Peter 4:10. Do you see how God has given each one of us different gifts? We're not all the same! God has given us gifts so that we can use them to help each other. Since Alexandra discovered her gifts, she started singing worship songs in choir. She also makes people happy as she entertains them through her plays.

Be brave enough to be yourself so that others can experience the unique gifts you bring to this world!

BECOMING BRAVE

Have you found your own unique talents or gifts? If not, ask your parents, teachers, pastors, or coaches to help you. It may take courage for you to try new things, but you've got it in you!

COURAGEOUS CALL

Dear Jesus, sometimes trying new things is hard. What if I am not good? What if others make fun of me? Help me to be brave and try new things. I know You will help me discover the unique gifts I have to offer the world. In Jesus' name, Amen.

I Can Stand Alone

CHAPTER 38

THE SUBSTITUTE SITUATION

scared, being alone

Mrs. Miller was out for the day which meant . . . substitute teacher! Aisha loved days when they had a sub. The subs were always nice and it usually meant an easy day of schoolwork.

This sub was one the class had never had before. Ms. Sneedy didn't smile one bit. Her list of things they had to do seemed longer than the Mississippi River. One of them was a surprise spelling test. Aisha was not prepared at all.

As her class headed outside for break time, the kids gathered together. "Ms. Sneedy isn't any fun!" one of the boys called out. "Yeah, so let's make up our own fun!" another chimed in. In a few short minutes, they had a plan to bring some silliness into the substitute teacher's day. One by one, each student would get up to sharpen their pencil, until Ms. Sneedy was flustered.

Just the thought of the plan made Aisha feel queasy. What if the teacher got really mad? What if she sent the names of the kids who did it to the principal? What if her parents found out? The thing that upset her the most was what if she was the only one who didn't participate and the other kids teased her? What if they kicked her out of the fun group and she was all alone?

As break time came to an end and the students went back into the building, Aisha struggled with what to do. She didn't feel like she could ask anyone else to not participate. She wanted to be courageous, but could she do it alone?

One of my favorite verses is Isaiah 41:10 (NLT) "Don't be afraid, for I am with you. Don't be discouraged, for I am your God. I will strengthen you and help you. I will hold you up with my victorious right hand." When I feel afraid and all by myself, I remind myself that I am never alone. God is always with me, giving me strength and helping me. There is never a situation when He isn't with me. He says He will hold us with His victorious right hand. That means He will!

As Aisha sat in class and watched the students get up one by one, her fears continued to fuel her anxiety. Then, Ms. Sneedy stepped in and made the students stop. Aisha's greatest fear didn't even happen and she felt calm one again.

GETTING TO KNOW YOU

(*Circle an answer below each question.*)

If Aisha had come to you, what kind of advice would you have given her:

a. Tell all the kids not to do this.

b. Just wait and see what happens.

c. It's not a big deal; just go along with it.

The thought of being the only one in a situation makes you feel:

a. Terrified.

b. Nervous, but you feel confident.

c. You've had to do it before and already know God is with you.

When you read God's Word and He says, "I am with you. I will strengthen you. I will help you" do you find:

a. Comfort.

b. Strength.

c. The need for more faith.

COURAGEOUS CALL

Dear Jesus, I feel afraid, especially when I may have to go against other kids and stand by myself. I want to remember that You say I am never alone. In Jesus' name, Amen.

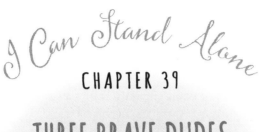

I Can Stand Alone

CHAPTER 39

THREE BRAVE DUDES

scared, being alone

King Neb, whose story is found in Daniel 3, made a ginormous golden statue of himself—as in 9 stories tall! Then he told all his people that they had to stand in front of his big statue. That wasn't enough, though. He took it even further and said if they didn't bow down before his statue, they would be thrown into a huge, superhot oven.

Picture this: a huge field crowded with people. Music begins to play. Everyone gets on their knees before the statue.

Except three guys.

Alone. Tall. Brave.

God told His people to never bow down to a statue. Shadrach, Meshach, and Abednego knew what God had said. They also knew they weren't going to do what it took to belong if it meant disobeying God.

Nebuchadnezzar was furious! He commanded that the guys

be brought to him and that they bow down. The three answered him: "King Nebuchadnezzar, we do not need to defend ourselves before you in this matter. If we are thrown into the blazing furnace, the God we serve is able to deliver us from it, and he will deliver us from Your Majesty's hand. But even if he does not, we want you to know, Your Majesty, that we will not serve your gods or worship the image of gold you have set up." Daniel 3:16–18 (NIV)

Shadrach, Meshach, and Abednego knew what the consequences were (being thrown into the blazing furnace) yet they still chose to follow only God.

Spunk. Grit. Guts. Whatever you call it, it is why these guys were able to answer Nebuchadnezzar ". . . we will not serve your god or worship your image." They had heard stories of their God's power, plus they had experienced God's help. They knew their God was the One True God and He was in control—not King Neb, the popular people, or anyone else.

Did their bravery mean they weren't scared? I doubt it.

Did they want to back down? I'm sure they did!

But they did not.

After they were thrown into the furnace, King Nebuchadnezzar leaped to his feet in amazement. "Weren't there three men that we tied up and threw into the fire?" he said. His advisors replied, "Yes." "Look! I see four men walking around in the fire, unbound and unharmed, and the fourth looks like a son of the gods," Neb declared.

When the guys had to be the bravest, they were not alone! When they went into the furnace, God was right there with them, protecting and helping them to be brave.

BECOMING BRAVE

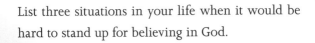

List three situations in your life when it would be hard to stand up for believing in God.

_____

_____

_____

COURAGEOUS CALL

Dear Jesus, I have never faced anything like these three brave men. I ask You to grow my faith and my fearlessness more and more as I learn to trust in You. I want to be that brave. In Jesus' name, Amen.

CHAPTER 40

PLEASE LIKE ME

friends, scared, peer pressure, standing alone

One day during fourth grade, my friend Liz asked me to come over after school. Now my mom had a rule that I couldn't go to anyone's house if there wasn't a parent there. Liz's parents both worked away from home during the day. I don't remember what I told my mom, I just remember going to Liz's house when her mom wasn't home. My mom had also told me to never mess around with cigarettes. I could hurt myself or start a fire. Liz said, "Let's give it a try." I wasn't like the three brave guys. I went along with her.

Why didn't I listen to my mom's wise advice?

I didn't listen because I wanted Liz to like me. I didn't want to be different.

At some point, you will find yourself in a situation similar to mine. It probably won't be exactly the same. It might involve a TV show, a computer, a movie, a video, a friend, or a boy. There will be pressure, just like King Neb put pressure on Shadrach, Meshach, and Abednego to bow down to his statue in Daniel 3.

If you don't do what your friends, or those you think are your friends, want you to do, what will happen?

Like for Shadrach, Meshach, and Abednego, there may be a cost.

Your friends might ignore you at lunch, walk away from you at recess, or leave you out of plans. They may take pictures without you, kick you out of the friend group, or cut you out of their group text.

So why be brave? Perhaps you've wondered.

Why shouldn't I do what everyone else is doing?

Why should I be different?

Why should I do what is right when wrong seems more fun?

Why would I be the kind one?

Why should I show love when people are mean to me?

Why should I be brave?

When God created you, he had a plan. Jeremiah 29:11 (NLT) tells us about those plans: "For I know the plans I have for you," says the LORD. "They are plans for good and not for disaster, to give you a future and a hope."

His plans are for your good. All too often, the path of following your friends will not lead to those good plans. If your friends are being sneaky or going against what is good, those plans can lead to your pain. I know it is hard to see that! You're just getting started on this journey called life. But the thing is, the steps you take today will take you to becoming someone—either a girl who finds God's best through obeying him or to a girl who can miss that best.

The girl who is brave finds God's best; His plans for good for her life. The girl who runs with the "in" crowd all too often will miss it.

BECOMING BRAVE

Grab a map or a globe. Look over the map or globe and choose a spot you would like to travel to. Now, in the space below, plan out your dream vacation. Where would you go? What would you do? How long would you stay? Just as you enjoy planning a "good" trip, God enjoys planning good for your life.

_____

_____

_____

_____

COURAGEOUS CALL

Dear Jesus, I am brave! I know I am because You are in me and You are brave. Help me to remember that each day I choose to be brave I am taking a step closer to Your best for me. In Jesus' name, Amen.

I Can Stand Alone

CHAPTER 41

PASSING THE TEST

friends, scared, peer pressure, standing alone

Right now you may have friends that you like to do fun things with. But as you get closer to becoming a teenager, things may change. It might start to feel like not everyone is going in the same direction as you. In fact, some friends might completely turn off the road of choosing what is right. They may start doing things that are not good. You may have fewer friends or for a time, you may feel alone.

You take tests in school, right?

When you take those tests, is your parent, teacher, or best friend sitting right with you giving you the answers? Of course not. That would be cheating!

The tests of our character—the tests that we are taking and passing to become a brave beauty—can be the same way. When we take these life tests we can feel alone.

Although we might not have another human right there with us when we have to be brave, God always is!

He makes this promise in Isaiah 43:2 (MSG), "When you're in over your head, I'll be there with you. When you're in rough waters, you will not go down. When you're between a rock and a hard place, it won't be a dead end—Because I am God, your personal God, The Holy of Israel, your Savior."

Passing tests isn't just a school thing, it's a life thing. Every day, our lives are full of tests, some small and some huge. Whether or not we keep moving forward, growing into a strong girl has to do with how well we do in those life tests.

When your friend asks to cheat off your paper, how will you react? It's an honesty test.

That party that comes and goes without you being asked. There's a joy test.

When you see the girl sitting alone. You see—but what do you do? It's a kindness test.

These tests, or choices, when added up, determine the girl you are growing into. Each and every day, you are growing. You are growing into a girl who is loving, joyful, kind, strong, and brave or you are growing into a girl who is the opposite.

What kind of a girl are you growing into?

BECOMING BRAVE

Grab some old magazines. Leaf through them and cut out words or pictures you would use to describe yourself. Hang them up on your door or wall as a reminder of the girl you are becoming.

COURAGEOUS CALL

Dear Jesus, I hadn't really thought about how I am growing in more ways than just my body. I want to grow to be brave. These life tests are hard, Lord. But I know that with Your help, I can pass them! In Jesus' name, Amen

CHAPTER 42

WHO? ME?

scared, being alone

What is the scariest thing you have ever had to do? The scariest thing I ever did I can actually blame on my youngest daughter, Madi. When she was thirteen years old, she asked if on her eighteenth birthday I would go skydiving with her. Skydiving, as in jump out of an airplane with a parachute. Since five years was a long way away; I just knew she would change her mind or forget. So jokingly I said, Sure! Laughing and joking, what I was really saying was No way! Who would really want to jump out of a plane?

Would you?

As Madi's eighteenth birthday got closer, she began using words like, "you promised" and that's when I started freaking out a bit. She really wanted to do this! So, I asked her brother Zak if he would jump out of a plane with his sister. When he said "yes," I felt much better. But when the big day came, her brother couldn't go. I knew someone had to go with Madi. I couldn't let her jump alone.

Madi turned eighteen . . . and I jumped out of a plane.

Have you ever needed to do something but you didn't have the bravery to do it? Try a new sport? Read a report in front of your class? Sing for a group of people? What are you supposed to do when you need to be brave, but you just aren't?

One thing I often do is write out verses and read them to myself over and over and over again. Verses like Psalm 27:1 (NLT) "The LORD is my light and my salvation—so why should I be afraid? The LORD is my fortress, protecting me from danger, so why should I tremble?"

GETTING TO KNOW YOU

(Circle an answer below each question.)

If you are in a tough situation and don't have the bravery you need, would you:

a. Ask someone else to do it for you, if they could.

b. Ignore the situation and hope it goes away.

c. Try to find the courage to do what you need to do.

When you're feeling stuck, you usually:

a. Get frustrated and give up.

b. Cry until you feel better.

c. Work hard to find an answer.

You most often feel like you need help when you:

a. Work on your homework.

b. Learn a new sport.

c. Do one of your chores.

With the help of a parent, you can see a picture of me skydiving on my Brave Beauty Scrapbook. Log onto my website: www.LynnCowell.com and click on the books tab. You'll find one for "Brave Beauty" there.

COURAGEOUS CALL

Dear Jesus, just thinking about this scary situation makes me nervous! I know you have promised to never leave me or forsake me. Help me remember that as I go forward! In Jesus' name, Amen.

I Can Do the Scary Things

CHAPTER 43

THE DAUGHTERS OF Z

scared: being alone

I think it is fun finding stories in the Bible I have never heard before, like the one about these gals, for example.

Actually, I'm not sure if I should call them women or girls because the Bible doesn't tell us how old they were. We find the story of the daughters of Zelophehad in the book of Numbers. Check out their names: Mahlah, Noah, Hoglah, Milcah, and Tirzah. Let's skip all that hard pronouncing and just call them the daughters of Z, ok?

You can read the story of the daughters of Z in Numbers 27. They were in a really tough situation. In ancient times, only men could own land. Usually, that wouldn't be a problem, because there would be men in the family to take care of the women. Their dad would provide until they were old enough to marry and then their husband would. If they didn't have either of those, it was their brother's responsibility.

The girls' problem was that they didn't have any men in their family; no dad, no brothers, no husbands, and no sons! Unlike today, the daughters of Z couldn't just go get a job and rent an apartment or buy a house. Since women couldn't own land, they would be homeless.

The daughters of Z had a choice. They could remain stuck in their problem or they could find the bravery they needed to do what no one else had ever done: ask for land to live on even though they were women.

The daughters made the courageous choice. They decided to go before the leaders of their community and ask for land. That would be kind of like us going to court today. They went to those in power: "Give us property." Their leader, Moses, then went to God to ask Him what to do and God said, "They are right! Give them land."

They were brave, did the scary thing, and got what they needed. What courageous girls!

BECOMING BRAVE

Based on the story of the daughters of Z, what do you think God's view on women and/or girls is?

COURAGEOUS CALL

Dear God, just thinking about my scary situation makes me want to run and hide. But I know if the daughters of Z could be brave enough to go speak to a panel of powerful men, with Your help, I can be brave too! Help me to always remember that You love and care about women, even when at times it seems like society doesn't. In Jesus' name, Amen.

I Can Do the Scary Things

CHAPTER 44

HOW DID THEY DO THAT?

scared, being alone

What was the last scary thing you did? How did you feel?

When I was in sixth grade, my church had a contest to see who could bring the most friends to church. Yes, I wanted to win, but I also wanted my friends to learn more about Jesus, who I had come to love. I was afraid to invite them, though. What if they thought I was weird for asking? What if they talked behind my back about how strange they thought I was? Finally, I got past the whirling worry in my head and went for it. I decided the worst that could happen would be that they said "no." I did it scared.

When I read stories of others who are courageous and do scary things, I see something that many of them have in common: they did it scared.

Most of them never overcame being scared, but that didn't stop them from being brave.

Shadrach, Meshach, and Abednego obeyed God rather than

Nebuchadnezzar and were thrown into a fiery furnace. I bet they were still scared, yet they obeyed God.

The daughters of Zelophehad were probably very scared to go to the powerful men and ask for land to live on, but they did it anyway!

Nicodemus went at night to ask Jesus questions about things he didn't understand.

Rhoda tried to convince the adults that Peter wasn't a ghost, but was really at the gate.

The woman at the well kept listening to Jesus even though He knew all about her sins.

They all did what they did even though they were probably shaking in their shoes!

Guess how many times the Bible says "fear not"? One translation has it 74 times. Seventy-four times God tells us to not be afraid. God told us "do not be afraid" so many times because He knows fear is a huge problem for us. While it might be normal, it is not what He wants for us. He wants us to be fearless.

Like all these Bible characters, finding the fearless you begins with finding faith in the God in you. By yourself, it is almost impossible to simply stop being afraid. When we teach ourselves the truth about the power that is within us, the same power that created the world and raised Jesus from the dead, that's when our faith makes us fearless!

Like Shadrach, Meshach, and Abednego said: "Our God is able!" (Daniel 3:17) It's not that they thought they were all that great; they knew their God was all that great. He can do anything. He is the one we can build our fearless faith on!

BECOMING BRAVE

Ask your mom or dad if you can listen to or download the song "More than Conquerors" by Rend Collective. Learn and sing the song whenever a scary thing comes up. Start singing the song out loud or in your head to remind yourself that you are more than a conqueror in Christ!

COURAGEOUS CALL

Dear Jesus, I often feel fearful, but I know You don't want that for me. No matter what I face, whether small or tall, I know that You are able to help me! In Jesus' name, Amen.

I Can Do the Scary Things

CHAPTER 45

DO IT AGAIN

scared, being alone

My daughter Mariah really wanted to be part of our state's honor choir. First, Mariah had to be chosen at her school. To be picked, she had to try out by singing a solo for her teacher. She was scared, but she really wanted to be a part of the choir. She made it!

Next, she traveled a couple of hours away and sang a solo in a room with five judges. We had to wait all day to see who had made it. When the list was posted, Mariah's name was not on the list. The disappointment she felt was overwhelming; she had worked so hard.

The next year, Mariah did it all again. Sang for her teacher. Traveled to the audition. Sang for the judges.

She didn't make it again. That was it; she didn't have an opportunity to try again.

Sometimes, even when we do the scary thing, it doesn't work out.

Mariah could have quit after the first time. Even after the second rejection, Mariah could have been done doing scary things. But you know what happened? After Mariah allowed herself some time to feel sad about her loss, eventually Mariah became even braver! Doing scary things prepared Mariah to be brave again and again. She knew if she could do it once, she could find the courage to do it again.

In Psalm 23 (NLT), David says, "Even when I walk through the darkest valley, I will not be afraid, for you are close beside me . . ." David didn't say, "If I walk through the darkest valley . . ." David knew life was hard. He also knew God was close beside him, so he would not be afraid.

When it doesn't go right the first time, you don't have to quit. You can be brave and do it again. You might have to try out for that sport twice. You may have to ask your teacher for that privilege more than once. You will probably have to be the one who asks the new friend over another time.

You can be brave because your bravery doesn't come from someone being your friend or someplace that makes you comfortable or something like your talents or your looks. Your courage comes from Christ. You have Christ Confidence!

Even if you are shaking, God isn't! You can have unshakeable courage in your unshakeable God.

Girls, we can't be courageous because of a best friend or a club we belong to or because of how pretty we are. We have to build our courage on God. He is the only thing that cannot be taken from us. He is the one thing that never changes.

BECOMING BRAVE

When was a time that you didn't make the team, failed a test, or had to try out again? What did you learn about the activity that you could take into your next experience? What did you learn about you?

Can you see how God redeemed your failure? Can you see good that came from the bad?

_____

_____

_____

_____

COURAGEOUS CALL

Dear God, I want courage that, even if I am shaking, I can know my unshakeable God is beside me. I trust you! Please help me with _____ (fill in the blank). In Jesus' name, Amen.

I Can Change

CHAPTER 46

HELP

changing, fear, power

I'm not quite sure how old I was when I started getting the remarks on my report card: *Lynn needs to learn how to be quiet.* I guess it was at whatever age I started getting report cards. I read them. I talked to my mom about the changes I needed to make. But when it came to actually making the change, I didn't.

I didn't change until the consequences were about to become huge.

Begging my parents for a wonderful opportunity, they allowed me to make the switch from a public school to a private school in seventh grade. I really enjoyed it, but my teachers were not enjoying me. My talkative ways were disrupting their classes. So, after my first semester I was given an ultimatum: find the self-control I needed or find a new school.

Now, my teachers had my attention. The question was: *Could I do it? Could I really have that much self-control?*

I wrote in my diary: "Lord, I really like this school, but I don't know if I can make this change. I really, really need your help."

Help. It's the one-word prayer God can answer.

The first thing I needed to understand in order to change was that I wasn't just disobeying my teachers. By disobeying my teachers, I was disobeying God.

Second, I needed to get that God understood that change was hard for me. He wasn't mad at me. He got me and He would help me.

Hebrews 4:13–16 (NLT) tells us, "Nothing in all creation is hidden from God. Everything is naked and exposed before his eyes, and he is the one to whom we are accountable. Christ is Our High Priest. So then, since we have a great High Priest who has entered heaven, Jesus the Son of God, let us hold firmly to what we believe. This High Priest of ours understands our weaknesses, for he faced all of the same testings we do, yet he did not sin. So let us come boldly to the throne of our gracious God. There we will receive his mercy, and we will find grace to help us when we need it most."

Do you see what I see? God understands our weaknesses. He is not mad at us; He gets us. That is why we can boldly come to Him as His daughters and bravely say, "Daddy, help!"

Jesus helped me. I learned the self-control I needed to keep my thoughts in my head until it was the right time to talk. I am so thankful I did. I got to stay at my school.

BECOMING BRAVE

Is there an area in your life you need to change? Reread Hebrews 4:13–16 in another Bible translation. Ask an adult or older sibling to help you use Biblegateway.com and try reading this verse in The Message. Are you surprised at the way God feels about our weaknesses?

COURAGEOUS CALL

Dear Jesus, help! In Jesus' name, Amen.

I Can Change

CHAPTER 47

POWER TO CHANGE

changing, fear, power

When Jesus was on earth, He had twelve guys He hung out with. He taught them about His Father, God, and God's ways. One of these guys was named Peter. Peter struggled with being scared and intimidated by others.

Luke 22:54–62 tells a story of Peter's fears getting the best of him.

Soldiers had arrived at the Garden of Gethsemane to arrest Jesus. Peter followed at a distance because he was afraid of them. When they arrived, sitting down by a fire in the courtyard, a young girl said to all those around, "This man also was with Jesus." But Peter denied it, saying, "I do not know Him." A little later someone else saw him and said, "You also are one of them." But Peter said, "Man, I am not." About an hour later another said the same thing. But Peter said, "Man, I do not know what you are talking about." While he was still speaking, the rooster crowed. Jesus turned and looked at Peter. Peter remembered that Jesus had told him that before the sun came up, Peter would deny that he knew Jesus three times. After this, Peter went out and wept bitterly.

Jesus wasn't unkind to Peter nor did He say anything to make him feel bad, but Peter knew he needed to change. Jesus had done so much for him and here Peter was, too afraid to even say he knew Jesus.

Can I tell you a secret?

I need to change too. I struggle with being stubborn. For many years my husband has told me that I am stubborn, but I didn't really believe him. Recently, I finally saw what he has been seeing and I decided: I am going to change.

It's been really hard! Not being stubborn means that instead of wanting things to go the way I think is best, I have to be flexible and reasonable to what others think is best. That doesn't sound too hard, does it? It is for me! Often the things I am stubborn about are things I want done my way because I am afraid of what will happen if they aren't.

Fear can cause us to act in ways we don't want. Jesus can help us change, even in the areas that are very hard.

After Jesus returned to heaven, just as He had promised, God sent the Holy Spirit to come and live inside of the disciples. The Holy Spirit gave Peter the power to change. He became one of the boldest preachers that ever lived. That is the power the Holy Spirit brings to me and you too, because when we invite Jesus into our lives, He lives in us as well!

BECOMING BRAVE

Ask the Holy Spirit to empower you to change.

COURAGEOUS CALL

Dear Jesus, change is hard for me. Please give me the power to change _____ _____ (fill in the blank). In Jesus' name, Amen.

I Can Change

CHAPTER 48

CHANGING IT UP

changing, fear, power

What is your favorite thing to drink in the morning? Chocolate milk? Orange juice? I'm a tea lover. This morning before I began to write, I heated up a cup of hot water so I could make some yummy hot tea. When the water was ready, I took the tea bag and pulled it up and down and up and down in the hot water. With each dunk of the tea bag, the clear water got a little bit darker, changing from clear water to tasty tea.

I once heard a pastor compare the changing of plain water to tea to our relationship with Jesus. My heart, which has been forgiven of my sins, is like the clear water. I spend time with Jesus, reading His words in the Bible, talking with Him through prayer, and learning more about Him by going to church. When I do, it's like the tea bag. As I get closer and closer to Jesus, He changes me. He makes me more and more like Him.

I wish that I could become like Him really fast, but sometimes there are things in my life that make it hard to change. Sometimes it's the thoughts I think about myself:

"I am too loud."

"I don't have what it takes."

"I am a disappointment to others."

These words don't always come from our own minds. Sometimes harsh words come from others such as teachers, friends, coaches, even our parents.

I'm discovering, as I learn what God says about me and I put His truth into my heart daily, change comes, like the tea bag.

When I think, "I am too loud" I remember God says I am perfect to Him. (Song of Solomon 5:2). If I feel like "I don't have what it takes" I remember God says in Hebrews 13:21 that He gives me everything I need. When someone says that I have disappointed them, I read that I am accepted by God. (Romans 15:7)

The Bible is full of many truths that help us: You are a child of God (John 1:12). You are a new creation (2 Cor. 5:17). You are set apart (Jeremiah 1:5). His word helps us to see what a treasure we are in Him.

When we read God's word, courageous becomes contagious! It starts changing all areas of our lives.

I'm beginning to believe: I am brave. I am confident.

And so are you, my friend!

BECOMING BRAVE

Pick one of the verses listed in the paragraph above and look it up in your own Bible. Underline it and keep it in a place where you can read it again.

COURAGEOUS CALL

Dear Jesus, I am excited to keep learning what You have to say about me. I know that what You say is true and that is what I want to believe about myself. In Jesus' name, Amen.

I Can Change

CHAPTER 49

COMING OUT OF THE DARK

fear, growing up

When Jenna was little, she was really afraid of the dark. At night when she heard noises, she would run to her parents' room and crawl into bed with them. After a while, her parents said she needed to learn to sleep on her own. So she created a pallet on the floor right by her door. That way if she needed them, she would be that much closer to her parents' bedroom.

That was when Jenna was little.

The problem was Jenna was older now and she was still scared of the dark. She was so afraid she didn't want to have sleep overs, go to Grandma's, or overnight camp. It was just too overwhelming for her.

Jenna didn't want to be afraid anymore, but the more she tried to be brave, the worse it got. She even had her mom pray with her each night. But the fears wouldn't go away. She began to feel like she would never change.

Matthew 19:26 (NIV) encourages us when we feel like it is

impossible to change, "Jesus looked at them and said, "With man this is impossible, but with God all things are possible." Jenna had lost hope, but God never does.

One thing that was making change hard for Jenna was that she was trying to change all at once. What she needed were small steps of bravery. Her first step was to sleep with a light on. That way she could see and not be afraid of what she couldn't see. She also got a noise maker to block out sounds that frightened her. She moved her furniture around so she could always see the door. One small step at a time, she became less afraid of the dark. Today, even though she is a teenager, she still uses a light, a noise maker, and has her bed facing the door. But those are all ok because for her, she is being brave.

BECOMING BRAVE

Do you have a fear in your life that you feel you should be over by now because you are growing up? Talk to an adult about your fear. See if they can help you take baby steps like Jenna to move toward the change you want.

COURAGEOUS CALL

Dear Jesus, my fears embarrass me sometimes. I don't want anyone to know because I don't want them to think I am a baby. Help me take small steps so that the impossible becomes possible in my life. In Jesus' name, Amen.

CHAPTER 50

WEARING BEAUTIFUL

beautiful, brave, being you

I always wanted to wear my older sisters' clothes. Theirs were cool; mine were not. At least that is the way I saw it.

They would get so mad at me when they discovered I had worn one of their shirts! I would have too. That really wasn't cool of me to take their stuff without asking. When my mom discovered what I was doing, oh, did I get in trouble.

Why would I risk getting my sisters mad at me and in trouble with my mom just so I could wear a shirt?

I wanted to be more like them and less like me. I wanted my friends to think I was cool . . . and a certain boy too!

What my friends thought about me was very important to me. I based how I felt about myself on what they said about me. When they said nice things, I felt great. When they didn't, I let their words make me feel bad.

Like the time my "friend" Dave called out, in the middle of our school hallway, "Lynn, why do you bother wearing a bra? You should just wear Band-aids." No "perfect" outfit was going to fix that comment!

I'm sorry to say too often the way I have felt about myself was all about how other people felt about me. I let other people define what beautiful looks like. Have you?

As I am growing in my relationship with Jesus, I am coming to trust what one person has to say about me: Jesus.

GETTING TO KNOW YOU

(Circle an answer below each question.)

How often do you think or worry about what you look like?

a. I look in the mirror a lot.

b. I do what I need to before I go somewhere, but that's about it.

c. Actually, I should probably pay more attention to my appearance.

When you are trying to decide what beautiful looks like, do you:

a. Look up to girls who are pretty outside *and* inside.

b. See what the girls at school do or wear.

c. Follow "pretty" people on social media.

As your body is starting to go through a lot of changes, how are these changes effecting the way you think of the word beautiful?

a. I think it is fun and I can't wait to be grown up.

b. It's ok. I'm not in a hurry, but I'm not afraid either.

c. It's hard for me to imagine calling myself beautiful.

COURAGEOUS CALL

Dear Jesus, I'm a bit confused right now about what beautiful is and what it is supposed to look like. Please help me to see beautiful the way You see beautiful. Then I know I'll have it right. In Jesus' name, Amen.

CHAPTER 51

BEAUTIFUL MEANS . . .

beauty, being you, brave

How would you define the word "beautiful"?
Maybe you have never thought about it before, but take a few minutes and once you have your answer, write it in the spot below. Don't be afraid. There is no right or wrong answer!

_____

_____

_____

I used to think beautiful was only what I could see with my eyes. I knew I wanted to be beautiful, but there really wasn't a whole lot I could do about it. You're born with what you're born with—or so I thought.

I wish someone had taught me when I was your age that beautiful is much more than what is on the outside.

There were two guys in Acts 3 who looked past what they could see on the outside of a person—their names were Peter and John. Peter and John went into the temple every day for prayer. Now there was a gate they had to pass through to get into the temple and that gate had a name. The gate's name was Beautiful because it was so pretty. I think it is very interesting that this gate was called Beautiful because you know what its purpose was? It separated those who could come in and those who couldn't and had to stay out. Like the ticket counter at the movies, not just any person could enter through the gate.

Every day, there was a crippled man who sat outside the gate going into the temple. He begged from the people who were coming in. When the crippled man saw Peter and John about to enter the gate, he asked them for money. Peter looked straight at him, as did John. Then Peter said, "Look at us!" So the man looked, expecting to get something from them.

Sometimes, you and I can be a bit like the crippled man at the gate. We are on the outside, or we feel like it. On the outside of the "in" group or the club for only those with certain talents. We might feel like we're on the outside from the kids who are super smart. (I always wanted to be in those classes for the "accelerated" kids.) We can feel on the outside based on so many things including where we live, where we go to school, what clothes we wear, or the color of our skin.

Like the crippled man, we may also want to beg from the "in" people. We can beg by posting only the perfect picture on our social media. We can beg by thinking if they would just invite me to their party or let me be on the team for the class project, I could finally belong. It's like we have our own gate called Beautiful, but it looks a bit different.

Friend, we don't have to beg. Our God, the One who made us, has already said we are beautiful, just the way we are. We don't have to change to be liked or do anything different to be loved. You are beautiful!

When the man looked up at Peter and John, ". . . Peter took the lame man by the right hand and helped him up. And as he did, the man's feet and ankles were instantly healed and strengthened. He jumped up, stood on his feet, and began to walk! Then, walking, leaping, and praising God, he went into the Temple with them." Acts 3:7–8 (NLT) That's what I call beautiful!

BECOMING BRAVE

On a separate piece of paper draw a picture of what the "Beautiful gate" might have looked like and think about how what others say is beautiful and what God says is beautiful can be so very different.

COURAGEOUS CALL

Dear God, thank you for these amazing stories in the Bible. Just reading them makes me feel like I can be brave. Thank you for people like Peter and John who didn't look at only the outside of the beggar, but looked at the beautiful person he was. I want to see the beauty not only in me, but in others too, Lord. In Jesus' name, Amen.

CHAPTER 52

YOU BELONG, BEAUTIFUL!

beauty, being you, brave

When I was your age, straight hair was in. That was great for me because my hair was stick straight. A few short years later, the rule was big is best! I got perms in my hair just to make it huge. In fact, one of my friends nicknamed me, "Lucy" as in Lucy from a cartoon called Peanuts. My hair looked just like Lucy's—black and curly.

In my tween years, bell bottoms were the bomb—the bigger the better. Oh, and make mine plaid, please! I had to have a pair of gauchos, too, in aqua blue with a little bit of yellow trim. By the time I got to junior high, bell bottoms were out. Skin-tight stirrups or parachute pants were the rage. Tight or tremendously loose, it didn't matter, just as long as you didn't have a bell at the bottom.

When I got to high school, I quit trying to keep up with the styles. Tired of trying to be like everyone else, I tried creating my own style. Not like anyone else, my style was me. Not everyone liked it; in fact, I was made fun of a time or two. But that didn't really matter to me. I was finally done with copying this girl or that one and over the exhausting drama of trying to be "in" (which I never truly achieved).

You can count on one thing when it comes to what's in: it will soon be out. Fashion is constantly changing—so fast it is hard to keep up.

It's not just what we wear, but how we look too! I didn't get braces until I was an adult. Yes, I was a little behind the times. One day while looking at a fashion magazine in the orthodontist office, I noticed something different about many of the models. They had a gap between their front teeth! Here I was, paying thousands of dollars to get my teeth nice and straight, and they were grinning with a huge gap.

Friend, you don't have to be a certain anything to be beautiful and belong. You are already beautiful, gap or no gap. Whether you are fashion forward or fashion behind, you will always belong!

BECOMING BRAVE

Ask your parent to buy you a poster board. Make a poster, just for you that says: "I am beautiful. I belong." Put this poster inside your closet door where you can read it every day when you get dressed.

COURAGEOUS CALL

Dear Jesus, I never really thought of myself begging, but I do know I desperately want to fit in and belong. Help me pay attention to my actions and the way I think. Help me remind myself I am beautiful to You even when I don't feel it. In Jesus' name, Amen.

CHAPTER 53

KIND IS THE NEW PRETTY

beauty, being you, brave, kindness

I bought a new T-shirt that I just love. It says, "Kind is the New Pretty."

It reminds me of my niece, Carley. Carley got an award for being kind. It came from her church, where she really wanted to be a volunteer. At her church you can't be a volunteer until you are in sixth grade. She was in third grade at the time. Carley looked for ways she could help out even when she wasn't an official volunteer. She was kind, even if others were mean to her. Because of the way she treated people, the adults at church began to trust her. They decided to give her a reward. Instead of having to wait three more years to volunteer, she only had to wait two! She got to begin volunteering in fifth grade. Carley was so excited. She said, "It is so cool to get a reward when you are not expecting it!"

Carley practiced putting her attention and energy into serving and being a blessing to other people instead focusing on herself.

Our society is very self-centered. Just look at the millions of selfies posted each day on social media. Jesus calls us to be other-centered instead of self-centered. Philippians 2:4 (NLT) tells us, "Don't look out only for your own interests, but take an interest in others, too."

This is so hard—putting other people first and serving their needs, concerns, and interests above our own. We can let the fear of missing out on fun or keeping up with popular people whisper in our ears. We can think: "If I don't focus on the fun and keep up with what is going on, I'll be left behind. Not everyone thinks being kind is cool."

But God does! He wants us to define beautiful the way he defines beautiful. Galatians 5:22–23 (NIV) tells us the traits that are found in a girl who is brave enough to build beauty into her life God's way: "But the fruit of the Spirit is love, joy, peace, patience, kindness, goodness, faithfulness, gentleness, self-control . . ."

This passage goes on to challenge us: "Let us not become boastful, challenging one another, envying one another." (NCV) (v.25)

Will you be brave enough to find your beautiful in Jesus?

BECOMING BRAVE

Think about the people around you. What inward traits make you want to be around them? What inner beauty makes them attractive? Then, pick one person. Create a card for her letting her know why you think she is so beautiful—on the inside.

COURAGEOUS CALL

Dear Jesus, what You call beautiful and what social media and society call beautiful can be very different. I want the type of beautiful that stays and grows more and more gorgeous each day as I become more like You. Help me to be brave enough to go after Your beauty. In Jesus' name, Amen.

CHAPTER 54
GOD STILL PERFORMS MIRACLES

faith, trust, confidence, believe, overcoming fear

At eight years old, Justine wasn't exactly sure what cancer was. But she did know her parents told her that her brother, Cappy, who was only eighteen months old, had this thing called cancer. She also knew that since her baby brother had cancer her mom, dad, and her baby brother often had to go away so that her brother could receive the special treatment he needed. Since this medical help was in another city, it often meant her parents were gone for several days in a row.

Justine may not have understood how serious this illness was, but she did understand one thing: her family needed God to heal her brother. God was big enough and had enough power. She believed God could and would heal Caspian.

Being the oldest of the four children in the family, Justine's sisters looked to her for strength and hope during this very hard time. While that is a big responsibility to carry for an eight year old, Justine helped her sisters to be brave while their parents were gone.

God answered their prayers; God did heal her brother. Yes, God performed miracles in the Bible and He still performs miracles today!

In Matthew 17:20 (NIV) Jesus says, ". . . Truly I tell you, if you have faith as small as a mustard seed, you can say to this mountain, 'Move from here to there,' and it will move. Nothing will be impossible for you." Jesus doesn't say that we have to have huge faith to see Him do big things. In fact, He says that if we only have faith the size of a tiny seed, nothing will be impossible for us.

Maybe there are times when you feel like because you are small, your faith is small. That is ok. Small people can see God do big things. Justine did!

GETTING TO KNOW YOU

(Circle one answer below each question.)

When you're in a situation that feels too big for you, what is the first thing you do?

a. Talk to my parent.

b. Share my feelings with God and ask him for help.

c. Worry about my problem and keep it to myself.

How do you feel about God still doing miracles today?

a. I know He does.

b. I believe He does, but I haven't had it happen to me.

c. I need more faith to believe like that.

Would any of these times be too long to pray for something?

a. A year.
b. Ten years.
c. A lifetime.

COURAGEOUS CALL

Dear God, I want to believe that You still do miracles today. Help me to believe in You for the miracle I need in my life. I trust You to do what is best for me and what will make Your name great to others too. In Jesus' name, Amen.

CHAPTER 55

BRAVE ENOUGH TO BELIEVE

faith, trust, confidence, believe, overcoming fear

Have you ever had an illness that just would not go away? The past couple of weeks I have struggled with a cold. I have taken vitamins and medicine. I've gotten extra sleep, yet I'm still sick. This cold is sticking around.

There was a woman in the Bible who had an illness that was much more than my little cold. Her story is told in Mark 5:25–34 (NIV). This woman had been bleeding for twelve years. Can you imagine? Twelve long years. She was completely worn out and beyond discouraged, not just from the physical pain, but the rejection. Her culture demanded that those who suffered from this type of condition couldn't live in the community; they had to live outside of town. Not only was her body broken, but her heart was too. "She had suffered a great deal under the care of many doctors and had spent all she had, yet instead of getting better she grew worse." (v. 26)

"When she heard about Jesus, she came up behind him in the

crowd and touched his cloak, because she thought, "If I just touch his clothes, I will be healed." (v. 27–28) (NIV) Immediately, Jesus' power went out of Him and into her. Her bleeding quit and her suffering stopped.

Jesus felt this powerful transaction. He wanted to know, "Who touched My clothes?"

The woman had shown great bravery when she made her way through the crowd and touched Jesus' clothing. She had shown confidence in God, believing she would be healed. She chose to be courageous, admitting the whole truth to Jesus. Jesus didn't want to know who touched Him because He was mad; He wanted to acknowledge her brave faith.

Some people think that believing Jesus can do big things, like heal us when we need it, is for people who are weak and can't do things on their own. Yet I believe we are courageous when we choose to trust God and believe He has the power to meet the needs we have. The woman extended her faith when she reached out her arm. God met her; her prayers were answered.

BECOMING BRAVE

There are some needs we have that society makes us feel rejected for, such as problems with our mind or emotions that can't be seen or physical problems that can be clearly seen but not understood completely. It takes a brave girl to notice and care for these people. Think of a person you know who is hurting. Take a moment to pray for him. Then choose one way you can let the person know he is cared for: make a card, send a text, or talk face-to-face.

COURAGEOUS CALL

Dear Jesus, I bravely ask You to heal _____
(fill in the blank with an area you need healing in or someone you know). I believe You were a healer when You were on earth, and I believe You still heal today. In Jesus' name, Amen.

CHAPTER 56

GO AND TELL

faith, trust, confidence, believe, overcoming fear

"Go and help others who need help" was the challenge Allie's church put out. A poverty-stricken mountain village in Jamaica needed the love of Jesus as well as work that would involve hands and feet.

Maddie, her sister, also had an opportunity to go and serve. Maddie's mission trip was to an impoverished community outside a large city in the United States.

Something tugged on the two sisters' hearts to go; they each believed this nudging was God speaking to them. Though they were young, they believed God could use them and wanted to use them.

Two opportunities. Two sisters.

Two problems.

Where would they get the money to go? The amount needed was a lot and asking Mom and Dad to pay for the trips just wasn't going to work.

The sisters prayed and asked God to help. They had faith that if

He was calling them to go, He would provide for them. Believing God would make a way, Allie and Maddie set out to raise the funds they needed. They dog sat and babysat; they even had a garage sale.

Just like they expected Him to, God came through. While they were doing what they could, God was doing what He could. He provided a way! Allie and Maddie earned enough money to go. Both girls had amazing experiences, helping people and sharing the love of Jesus.

In Paul's letter to the Philippians, he provides this encouragement, "And my God will meet all your needs according to the riches of his glory in Christ Jesus." Philippians 4:19 (NIV)

God knows we have needs. He allows us to have needs so that we realize we need Him. Not being able to do things completely on our own requires us to have faith and trust. Trusting God, rather than trying to do everything on our own, builds our faith so that we **can** do things that would be impossible on our own.

I know you may not be old enough to go on a mission trip, but you can still be encouraged by the stories of girls just a few years older than you. Now is the time for you to become brave and believe God will meet every need you will have in serving Him.

BECOMING BRAVE

What is one way you can do something for God now? Is there a nonprofit you know of that you could raise money for? Does your family sponsor a child in another country that you could write to? You may be young, but you can begin doing big things now. A big God lives in you!

COURAGEOUS CALL

Dear God, I like the idea of not waiting until I am older to begin making a difference in my community and sharing Your love. Help me find just the right fit, where I can be a blessing to others and help them to see You. In Jesus' name, Amen.

CHAPTER 57

NEVER TOO YOUNG TO BELIEVE

I Am Brave Enough to Believe

faith, trust, confidence, believe, overcoming fear

Years and years and years of dreams; that is what my pile of diaries are filled with, beginning when I was just eight years old.

One of the most bravery-building things I do is go back and read the dreams I wrote about to see how God has come through on those dreams that I had that I later began to pray for.

When I was in third grade, I wanted to be a children's book illustrator. My love of books was just beginning. Later, I asked God if I might write a book one day. Right now I am writing my fifth book.

I dreamed of marrying a pastor one day. I thought that would be the best way for me to share and spread the love of Jesus. Instead, Jesus had me become a speaker, so I teach the good news of Jesus to others.

As I read my journals, I see how God answered my prayers. But there is a difference between what I prayed and how He answered. Ephesians 3:20 (NIV) explains: "Now to him who is able to do immeasurably more than all we ask or imagine, according to his power that is at work within us, to him be glory in the church and in Christ Jesus throughout all generations, for ever and ever! Amen."

Wow! Do you see what I see? God is able to do immeasurably more than you and I can ask or imagine. Another version says, "God can do anything, you know—far more than you could ever imagine or guess or request in your wildest dreams!" Ephesians 3:20 (MSG) Whatever big thing you can dream, God can do bigger.

How?

He accomplishes big things through us because of his power in us. You will not do great things because you are so great. You are great because the One who is in you is great. He will do the great things through you.

Why?

He chooses to do amazing things through me and you so that others will see Him. Not so that people would one day say, "That Lynn, she is a good writer and speaker." It is not so that we can have tons of likes and followers on social media. God's not into that. Too often social media is all about making us feel good and important. That is not why we are here or why we were created. We were made for one purpose: to make God famous. To point others to the way, the truth, and the life: Jesus.

This is not the dream or goal of most people. That's why you are going to be different. That is why you've got to be brave; brave enough to believe God has a big purpose for you. When you and He partner together, there is nothing He can't do through you!

BECOMING BRAVE

Take a moment to think of something that you might do for God one day; something that seems very big. Write this dream down.

_____

_____

_____

_____

COURAGEOUS CALL

Dear God, place in my heart big dreams of what You can do through me. In Jesus' name, Amen.

I Am Truthful

CHAPTER 58

HERE IS WHAT HAPPENED

honesty, truthful, real

Carley knew the right thing to do, but she really didn't want to do it.

A classmate had her phone out a few minutes after she wasn't supposed to. The teacher got angry with her and the girl got in trouble. It was her last warning that day and at that point, the teacher said she was going to call her parents. Carley knew it was really Carley's fault. She had told her classmate that they could keep their things out. Carley knew the right thing to do was to take the blame for it. She told the teacher she thought they could keep their things out longer and had told her friend. The great thing is that when Carley spoke up and was truthful, neither one of the girls got in trouble.

Psalm 28:7 (NIV) tells us, "The LORD is my strength and my shield; my heart trusts in him, and he helps me. My heart leaps for joy, and with my song I praise him."

When Carley did the right thing and spoke truthfully, the Lord helped her. The situation even turned out the way Carley and her classmate would have wanted. The result was that both girls were happy.

The Old Testament part of the Bible was written in the Hebrew language. In this verse the word "heart" in the Hebrew language means: courage, mind, or understanding. The word "trusts" means: rely on, put confidence in, to be confident. If we plug those words into our verse to help us understand it even more, it could sound like this: The Lord is my strength and my shield; I receive courage in my mind when I rely on him and become confident.

It is hard to be honest, especially when telling the truth can get you in trouble. When we do the right thing, it might not always turn out the way that we want, but God promises to give us the courage we need to do the right thing. We don't have to do it alone. Whether the outcome is what we wanted or not, He can help us still feel peaceful knowing we did the right thing.

GETTING TO KNOW YOU

(*Circle an answer below each question.*)

When do you find it the most difficult to be truthful?

a. With my teacher.
b. With my parents.
c. With my friends.

Do you most struggle to be honest when you are afraid of:

a. Getting in trouble.

b. Someone not liking you.

c. Being left out.

Why do you think Jesus wants us to be truthful *(you can pick more than one)?*

a. Because lying can hurt other people.

b. Lying makes relationships difficult.

c. Lying makes people not trust each other.

COURAGEOUS CALL

Dear Jesus, it is hard to be honest and truthful all the time. Sometimes it's not so much that lying is the struggle, but not speaking up when I know the truth. Keep my conscience soft and help my courage to be strong. In Jesus' name, Amen.

CHAPTER 59

HALF-TRUTH OR WHOLE TRUTH

honesty, truthful, real

Is a half-truth still the truth or is a half-truth a lie?

Abram (that was his name before God changed it to Abraham) was in a sticky situation. There was a famine in the land he was living in. He needed to make a move to get his family food before they starved. Word was out that there was food in the nearby country of Egypt. So they loaded up and headed out.

"As he was approaching the border of Egypt, Abram said to his wife, Sarai, "Look, you are a very beautiful woman. When the Egyptians see you, they will say, 'This is his wife. Let's kill him; then we can have her!' So please tell them you are my sister. Then they will spare my life and treat me well because of their interest in you." Genesis 12:11–13 (NLT)

Abram was right. When they arrived in Egypt, the Egyptians thought Abram's wife was so beautiful they brought her to Pharaoh. It looked as though Pharaoh would make her his wife!

Pharaoh was so happy with Sarai, he gave Abram, who he thought was her brother, many wonderful gifts.

The Lord was angry with Pharaoh for taking Sarai so He brought diseases on Pharaoh's house. Then Pharaoh knew the truth! "So Pharaoh summoned Abram and accused him sharply. "What have you done to me?" he demanded. "Why didn't you tell me she was your wife? Why did you say, 'She is my sister,' and allow me to take her as my wife? Now then, here is your wife. Take her and get out of here!" Genesis 12:18–19 (NLT)

Abram told a half-truth; he and Sarai were related. The whole truth was that Sarai was already married. This half-truth, which was no truth at all, got Sarai in one big mess! Abram's lack of courage caused his family to have to leave the land where there was food and go back to the famine.

BECOMING BRAVE

Get some people together and create a play with the characters Abram, Sarai, and Pharaoh. Scene I is Sarai being taken to Pharaoh. Scene II is Pharaoh finding out Sarai is already married. Scene III is Abram and Sarai heading back to their country. After your play, talk about what Abram could have done in this situation to be fearless instead of fearful.

COURAGEOUS CALL

Dear Jesus, like Abram, I am tempted to not tell the whole truth when I think it will get me in trouble. Burn in my heart the story of Abram. Help me remember that the consequences of getting kicked out of Egypt not only impacted Abram, but his entire household. Help me be brave! In Jesus' name, Amen.

I Am Truthful

CHAPTER 60

MAKE THE RIGHT CHOICE

honesty, truthful, real

Ella couldn't sleep at night and her stomach had been hurting for days.

She had broken one of her family's technology rules, watching a video she knew was wrong. Being ten was hard sometimes. She knew the right thing to do, but since she knew how to do the wrong thing, it made obeying that much harder!

Now, she was having trouble sleeping. The anxiety and fear she felt over how her dad and mom would react when they found out overwhelmed her. She decided she couldn't take it anymore. She went to her mom, sobbing, and confessed what she had done wrong.

This step was a big one for Ella. Never before had she gone to her parents on her own when she had done something wrong; usually she waited until she got caught.

Ella was completely shocked by her mom's reaction. Her mom hugged her and thanked her for being honest. She told Ella how brave she was to come and tell the truth. Her mom let her know that she never wants Ella to be afraid to tell the truth even if telling the truth means revealing a previous lie. Her mom promised that she would not overreact or get angry with her. That didn't mean her mom would never be disappointed in her nor did it mean that honesty was a guarantee there would be no consequences or punishment for her actions. It did mean that her mom would help her to set things right when she needed it.

Ella was surprised and relieved. Being truthful was not as scary as she thought! She decided that going forward, she would choose to bravely be honest each time.

The Bible calls the relief Ella experienced peace and freedom. When we choose the truth, it sets our heart free from guilt and shame. Truth and freedom are found when we choose Jesus' way of handling difficult situations.

John 8:32 (NLT) says, "And you will know the truth, and the truth will set you free." The most important truth we need to know is that Jesus died to forgive us for our sins. When we make wrong choices, He will forgive us when we ask. Knowing that truth and choosing to ask Jesus for His forgiveness, gives us the relief we need from the way sin makes us feel—heavy, sad, and awful. Choosing truth sets us free!

BECOMING BRAVE

Come up with a story in which the main character has to be brave and be honest. In the story, tell how your character finds the courage to do the right thing.

_____

_____

_____

_____

COURAGEOUS CALL

Dear Jesus, when I make a wrong choice, it is so hard to do the right thing. Holy Spirit, help me to be brave and choose truth over a lie every time. In Jesus' name, Amen.

I Am Truthful

CHAPTER 61

KEEP IT TO YOURSELF

honesty, truthful, real, gossip

Kicked out of their house? Yes, that is what Kelly had said. Kayley's family was having some kind of financial problems so her family was moving. They couldn't pay for their house anymore. At least that is what Kelly told Josie.

Why hadn't Kayley told her? Josie wondered. They were really good friends. Kayley had told Josie she was moving, but she didn't say it was because they were being evicted from their home. Josie just had to tell all their friends; they would want to know too.

Later that afternoon, Josie spotted Kayley walking alone during break time, crying. *She must be crying because she is getting kicked out of her house. I would be crying too*, thought Josie.

Walking up to Kayley, Josie asked, "Kayley, what's wrong?" "I have no idea why or how it happened, but everyone keeps coming up to me asking me why my family is being evicted from our home. We're not. My dad got a promotion, so we are moving to a bigger house. I just don't understand how that rumor got started.

Why would someone make up such a thing?" she said through her tears.

Josie's face turned red. Why had she told others about Kayley's family? Even if it was true, which it wasn't, having others know of her family's finances would have hurt Kayley. Josie asked Kayley to forgive her for spreading what she never should have, especially when it wasn't even true.

Proverbs 16:28 tells us: "A dishonest man spreads strife, and a whisperer separates close friends." You and I might never think of ourselves as dishonest; it sounds so harsh. Yet that is exactly what we are if we choose to share information that we are not even sure is true. Not only that, but when we choose to sin by telling stories about others, we spread strife as Proverbs says. We take part in creating fights and conflict.

When you choose to not be a part of spreading strife, you are choosing the right way. You are choosing to be brave God's way.

BECOMING BRAVE

Think of the last time you heard a story about someone that was unkind. Did you stop to find out if the story was true? Why or why not?

COURAGEOUS CALL

Dear Lord, I don't want the reputation of being a girl who is dishonest. I want to be the one others can trust, no matter what. Knowing that is the girl I want to become, when the opportunity to be dishonest comes up, help me choose the opposite: honesty. In Jesus' name, Amen.

I Can Do It Scared

CHAPTER 62

DO IT SCARED

fear, courage, obeying God

My youngest daughter Madi was in fifth grade when she started traveling with me when I spoke at events. Often, at the end of the conferences, she and I would do a question and answer time with girls and their moms. While on stage, Madi would light up. Her passion to encourage girls to run to Jesus could not be contained once she got on stage.

Before Madi got on stage, she was terrified though. The uncomfortable feelings swirling inside her were overwhelming.

After a particularly powerful evening at one event, Madi informed me that although she had considered it, she could never be a speaker. "Why? You seem so natural when you are sharing!" I wanted to know.

"Every time I get ready to speak I get scared! Whether I'm with you or in a classroom at school, I feel like I can't do it." "Is that all?" I joked back with her.

Even after speaking for many years, I still have to do it scared. Right before I get ready to speak, my body tries to send me all kinds of signals. It's as if my mind and body are working together against me, trying to get me to stay in my seat. "You really have to go to the bathroom!" "Do you even remember your opening story?" "What if someone falls asleep in the middle of your message?" These fear-filled thoughts I have are not just made up. All the messages my mind sends to me come from very real experiences I have had. Once as I began my message, my hands and forearms went completely numb!

When I am in my seat getting ready to share a message, I have to remind myself, God has given me this opportunity and He will help me to do it. I have to tell myself that I want to honor Him and obey Him more than I fear people rejecting me.

Just because we feel afraid that doesn't mean that what we are about to do is not something God wants us to do, like me when I am getting ready to speak. Being fearful is not always an indication that we are not supposed to do something brave for God.

Sometimes we feel fearful because we don't want to fail or look like a fool. The fearful feelings we have try to be louder than our faith that God can use us. We have to remind our heart of the times God has helped us in the past; it forgets.

Like the time I just kept right on speaking while a bat flew around the room. Yep, God was there and He helped me. Then there was the time I had to stop and start a message because of a fire drill right in the middle of it. I also remind myself of when a woman passed out during my talk and some ushers had to come and carry her out. God was there for both of us!

Yes, these times were hard, but God was there.

GETTING TO KNOW YOU

(Circle an answer below each question.)

How do you feel about speaking in front of people?

a. I find it fun!

b. It's ok.

c. It terrifies me.

When have you had to "do it scared"?

a. Play an instrument in front of people.

b. Start a new school.

c. Fill in the blank _____

Which of these would be the scariest for you?

a. Trying a new sport.

b. Reading a report in front of your class.

c. Getting sick at school.

COURAGEOUS CALL

Dear Jesus, I need to learn to do it scared. I want to learn how to take the first step, knowing that no matter how frightened I feel, You are with me and You are helping me. In Jesus' name, Amen.

CHAPTER 63

MORE NAMES WE CAN'T PRONOUNCE

fear, obeying God, obedience, courage, faith

I found a story in the Bible that doesn't get told much, probably because the names are so hard to pronounce.

Take a few minutes and read Exodus 1:15–17.

I've never received a call or command from the head of a country. The closest I've ever come is receiving a phone call from my boss. And while that has only happened to me a couple of times, both times I immediately panicked. For no reason whatsoever, my mind immediately runs toward fear. *What did I do? Why is she calling?* Before I can push that red button to answer, my heart is on fire!

Do you know, every time the call has only been positive?

The women in this passage, Shiphrah and Puah, unlike me, had every reason to be terrified. Pharaoh, the ruler of Egypt was ruthless. These two women were midwives—they were trained to help women through childbirth. Pharaoh was trying to get rid of the Israelite people. His plan? Command the women to kill the little baby boys when they were born.

These women didn't care who was making the command. They feared God and did not do what the king of Egypt told them to do. They let every baby live; girl or boy.

Pharaoh knew what they were doing. He called the women to the palace to try to intimidate them into obeying him rather than God.

God had given these women a gift and a job to do: help bring God's babies into the world. A choice must be made. Shiphrah and Puah needed to make up their minds before they received their next patient's call—who would they obey?

Fear was going to be the driving force behind their decision. The question was who were they going to fear?

Exodus 1:17 says the women "feared God." Wait a minute? Through this whole book we have been saying fear is a bad thing. The Hebrew word used for fear here is *yare*. It means to be afraid, be frightened, to revere, to respect, or to be awesome. What the women felt toward God was respect and awe because of His power and holiness.

Yes, Shiphrah and Puah, were struck with awe, but not by the powerful intimidation of Pharaoh. Their fear, directed toward their awesome God, would empower them to become courageous.

Pharaoh packed a powerful punch, but it had the opposite effect of what he intended. His command brought out, from a place deep within, a faith deeper than the women's fear of the ruthless ruler, Pharaoh. Faith, that the God who had brought them safely to Egypt in the famine, would not quit on His promise to make them a great nation. Shiphrah and Puah chose to obey God over fearing Pharaoh.

"Do it scared" would become their motto.

God would come through just as Hebrews 6:10 (NIV) says: "God is not unjust; he will not forget your work and the love you have shown him as you have helped his people and continue to help them."

BECOMING BRAVE

Like two magnets, when it came to fulfilling the work God had given them to do, Shiphrah and Puah stuck together and did it scared.

Make a magnet to help remind you to do it scared. You'll need:

- A sheet of magnets
- Colored paper
- Markers

Write in your favorite color "Do it Scared." Finish decorating the paper any way you like and then attach it to the magnet by either peeling off the adhesive side if it has one or using glue. Stick the magnet on the inside of your locker at school or anywhere to remind yourself to "Do it Scared."

COURAGEOUS CALL

Dear Lord, being scared is no reason to not do the right thing. Help me to remember these courageous women and that I can also do it scared. In Jesus' name, Amen.

I Can Do It Scared

CHAPTER 64

LET'S ENJOY NOW

fear, obeying God, obedience, courage, faith

Where did all the fun go? Lately, when getting ready for school, Kennedy felt sad. There was just too much drama at school. Watching her two older sisters, she knew middle and high school had enough of that. She just wanted to enjoy this last year of elementary school without all that stuff.

Her parents, and even the school counselor encouraged Kennedy to bravely share how she felt with Crystal, the gal creating the latest drama. But what if Crystal didn't see it the way Kennedy saw it? What if instead she caused even more trouble and this time Kennedy was the center of it?

Kennedy decided to take the risk and go for it. She shared with Crystal what the rest of the year could look like if they all made up their minds to have fun—leave the daily drama behind. Crystal agreed. In fact, when it was over, it seemed to Kennedy that Crystal liked her more than before. Her courage paid off!

There was a guy in the Bible named Joshua who also had to

"do it scared." God had called him to move a million people into a new land. The problem was those who currently lived in the land had a reputation for being fighters. (They would make the drama at school look like a piece of cake.)

Here is what God said to Joshua, "Have I not commanded you? Be strong and courageous. Do not be afraid; do not be discouraged, for the LORD your God will be with you wherever you go." Joshua 1:9 (NIV)

Kennedy was scared to talk to Crystal, but she did it anyway. The same with Joshua. God commanded him to be strong and courageous. God said not to be afraid and that he would be with him, but that doesn't mean that suddenly Joshua was no longer scared.

When you step out and do the brave thing, you usually don't know how it will turn out. But here is the thing we always know: God is with us wherever we go. No matter where that is, He is going with us. Since He has made us this promise, we can gain the courage we need to be strong and not afraid or discouraged. He is with us and He will help us!

BECOMING BRAVE

Maybe God wants you to step up and bravely show leadership like Kennedy. The first step is the hardest, but like Kennedy and Joshua, God will be with you. Try talking with a parent, a coach, or a school counselor for some ideas on how you can show leadership.

COURAGEOUS CALL

Dear God, just thinking about talking to _____
(fill in the blank) makes my stomach spin. I need Your
help to get through this. Help me to know when and
how to step up and have the hard conversation I need to.
In Jesus' name, Amen.

I Can Do It Scared

CHAPTER 65

A NOTE FROM ABBY

fear, obeying God, obedience, courage, faith

Abby was nervous, as in shaking-in-her-shoes scared. She knew she wanted to try out for the Contest Company for her dance team, but that didn't mean she wasn't terrified. Now, after going through something so hard, Abby wanted to share with you how she got through.

Hey, Friend!

We all have challenges in life, right? But, how do you approach them? Many of us do it scared. Recently, I tried out for the Contest Company for my dance team. I was completely petrified. My hands were shaking and palms were sweating. You know the feeling!

How do we do scary things confidently? Well, there are many ways that you can calm your nerves!

Step One: trust what God has in store for you is the BEST! Even if it isn't what you wanted.

Step Two: take a deep breath. Breathing is crucial. Hey, you wouldn't be able to live without it!

Step Three: PRAYER! Prayer is a perfect way to calm your nerves and talk to God.

Next time you're nervous, scared, or having a nervous breakdown, talk to God, breathe, and trust.

XO,

Abby☺

The three steps Abby shared are helpful. God's word backs up her advice. "But blessed is the one who trusts in the LORD, whose confidence is in him. They will be like a tree planted by the water that sends out its roots by the stream. It does not fear when heat comes; its leaves are always green. It has no worries in a year of drought and never fails to bear fruit." Jeremiah 17:7–8 (NIV)

When we choose to trust God with situations beyond our control, confidence comes. We know God has what's best for us. No matter how our scary situation turns out, we can be peaceful. He's got us!

When we choose to trust God, this verse compares us to trees. My daughter Madi loves trees. She has a gigantic stretched canvas, a tapestry, a journal, and a wooden ornament all of trees. Madi's trees are reminders that in God, we are secure. Like tree roots, our security goes deep. Disappointment and discouragement don't cause us to shrivel or die. In fact, like the verse says, when "heat comes," which mean the hard times, our security in God goes even deeper as we depend on him.

When Abby wrote this letter, she still didn't know whether she made the team or not. If she does, how wonderful! If she does not, her confidence will continue to grow stronger. Her confidence doesn't come from a group; her confidence is built on love coming from her perfect Father God.

BECOMING BRAVE

Just like Abby did for you, take a moment to write a note to someone who needs your encouragement to be brave. That person might even be yourself!

COURAGEOUS CALL

Dear Jesus, teach me to trust You. Even when, especially when, things don't turn out the way I want them to. In Jesus' name, Amen.

SECTION 3

I AM CONFIDENT

CHAPTER 66

WHAT'S UP YOUR FAMILY TREE?

family, salvation, choices

You may not think it's a big deal, but the family you are growing up in is a big part of the girl that you already are and the person that you are becoming.

Want to take a look up my family tree?

I have a mom, stepdad, three brothers, four sisters, all their spouses, and twenty-one nieces and nephews. Many of my nieces and nephews are now married and they have babies too. My family is huge!

When I think about all of these people in my life (and there are a lot of them) I know that who I am today has to do with this big, beautiful family I am part of.

When you think of your family, can you see how part of who you are is also because of them? Whether you are the oldest, youngest, or somewhere in between, your family is playing a big part in the girl you are growing up to be.

Sometimes the way our family impacts us is wonderful. Home

may be a place where we feel loved and accepted. It is where we know no matter what else is going on around us or in our day, home is our safe place. We don't have to worry about someone bullying us or not including us.

Sadly, at other times, home is not the place we wish it was. Maybe death or divorce has brought pain to your family. Each weekend you feel sad as you move from one house to the other in order to spend time with those you love.

God is the one who created families from the very beginning, with Adam, Eve, Cain, and Abel. It says in Psalm 68:6 (NLT), "God places the lonely in families . . ." He desires our families to be a place of safety. Sometimes that means He needs to heal them so that they can become that place.

GETTING TO KNOW YOU

(Circle one answer below each question.)

When someone says the word "family," you think of:

a. Your parents, siblings, grandparents, aunts, uncles, cousins.

b. A community such as your neighborhood, church, or group of family friends.

c. God and the family of God.

The word "family" makes you feel:

a. Safe

b. Sad

c. Comfortable

One day, you would like to:

a. Get married.

b. Have children.

c. Both.

COURAGEOUS CALL

Dear Jesus, thank you for the family You have given me. I know it is not perfect, but I am still thankful for it. In Jesus' name, Amen.

CHAPTER 67

HE NEVER LOST

family, salvation, choices

Joseph's story begins in Genesis 37. Joseph had dreams he believed came from God. In these dreams, Joseph became a very powerful man. Joseph made the mistake of telling these dreams to his brothers. Because of the dreams and also because he was their dad's favorite, Joseph's brothers were very jealous, so they sold him as a slave. And so Joseph lost his family.

In Egypt, Joseph's purchasers sold him again, now to become a worker. He lost his home.

At his new job, his employer accused him of committing a crime he didn't commit. Thrown into prison, Joseph lost his reputation and it looked like his future.

You know one thing Joseph never lost?

Joseph never lost his confidence or his courage.

Joseph's confidence was the one thing he didn't lose because Joseph never lost his trust in God. That is exactly what the definition of confidence is: full trust; belief in the powers, trustworthiness, or reliability of a person or thing. (Dictionary.com)

Joseph never quit trusting that even through all of the hard stuff, God was with him.

Even though Joseph's family was unstable and even hurt him, he found God to be his safe place. He found an unshakeable confidence in an unshakeable God.

It took many years, but God used the confidence He built into Joseph to help rebuild Joseph's family. After losing his family, his home, and his reputation, God performed a miracle. Joseph became second in charge of all of Egypt. There was a famine in the land where his family lived, so his brothers went to Egypt to get food. Who was the person Joseph's brothers had to ask for food? Joseph. God helped Joseph forgive his brothers. God used him to bring healing to his family. (You can read the ending of his whole story in Genesis 41–47).

BECOMING BRAVE

When we lose something or someone or have things taken from us, it can cause us to be afraid of what might happen in the future. We learn from Joseph, no matter what happens, we can keep trusting God.

COURAGEOUS CALL

Dear God, Joseph's life was really hard! If he can find courage in You to be confident, I know I can too. You can do anything. I love you. In Jesus' name, Amen.

My Family

CHAPTER 68

WHY DO WE HAVE TO?

family, salvation, choices, changes

I sat in my backyard, staring at the house that would no longer be **my** home. I loved that place; it was the only home I had ever known.

Our neighborhood was a wonderful place to grow up. I could walk less than a block to school. My best friend lived next door. Living in the big house meant a bedroom of my own. Moving to the smaller, newer house meant a bedroom shared with my sisters. Moving meant my friend would not be next door and my new school would be a long walk from home.

Gazing at all I would lose, sadness swirled around in my heart. I didn't want to leave what I loved. Why would my parents make me go through this change? We didn't have to move. My dad wasn't switching jobs or making any other change requiring us to move. We were moving because my parents wanted to. Didn't they care that I didn't?

Unlike my move across town, Kari and Karla had to move out of state. Though they were scared, they chose to face their situation with courage and confidence. Even though it was intimidating, Kari and Karla knew God was them! At their new school He helped them to meet new friends and make a fresh start.

As a young girl, the changes resulting from moving took me by surprise. Ecclesiastes 3:1 (NIV) tells us, "There is a time for everything, and a season for every activity under the heavens." I didn't know that change was normal because I hadn't had many changes in my life. I didn't prepare my heart to be flexible, ready to make changes when changes are needed.

There is a time for everything including family changes and often these changes are hard.

No matter what comes, God tells us in every season, "Be strong and courageous. Do not be afraid or terrified because of them, for the LORD your God goes with you; he will never leave you nor forsake you." Deuteronomy 31:6 (NIV)

Change will come into your life and into your family. But you can know and be confident of this: your God is with you. Always. No matter where you go or what you do, you are never, ever alone.

BECOMING BRAVE:

What is the hardest part of being in your family? For every hard thing, write something good about being in your family.

THINGS THAT ARE HARD ABOUT MY FAMILY	THINGS THAT ARE GOOD ABOUT MY FAMILY

COURAGEOUS CALL

Using the chart above, create your own prayer, thanking the Lord for the parts of your family life that are good and asking Him for help where your family life is hard.

My Family

CHAPTER 69

ONE UP YOU

family, choices, loving difficult people, maturing

Every time they got together, Kelly's cousin Peyton needed all of the attention and that holiday weekend was no different. Not only did Peyton want everyone to pay attention to her, but no matter what Kelly did, Peyton had to do it too. Plus, she always tried to "one up" Kelly. When Kelly would tell a story, of course Peyton had done that too—only better. Kelly was worn out with it. She just wanted Peyton to go home so she could get back to her own life. In the meantime, Kelly held on to her confidence and let Peyton do what Peyton did. Letting Peyton get under her skin would only mean Kelly would be joining Peyton's childish ways. That's not what Kelly wanted; she wanted to grow into the girl who was not intimidated by another's insecurity.

Throughout the weekend, Kelly was holding her own, but it was hard not to let Peyton get under her skin! Throughout each day, she prayed silently for the Lord's help to not respond in a mean way. Talking it over with her mom also helped her to have the right perspective and to keep bravely doing the right thing. In the end, Kelly's choices helped turn the weekend into a nice one after all.

That long weekend, though she may not have realized it, Kelly was learning the truth of 2 Corinthians 5:12 (NIV), "We are not trying to commend ourselves to you again, but are giving you an opportunity to take pride in us, so that you can answer those who take pride in what is seen rather than in what is in the heart." Kelly could have turned that holiday into a competition with her cousin. Who did what first and who could do it better could have been the theme. That is not what Kelly did. Kelly did the hard work of growing her heart that holiday.

BECOMING BRAVE

Do you have a family member that is particularly hard to get along with? Take some time today to do a hard thing: say something nice about them. Think of one positive thing about this person and then write a card, give a call, text, or post something nice on their social media.

COURAGEOUS CALL

Dear Jesus, I find it really hard to get along with _____. Like 2 Corinthians 5:12 says help me to focus on what is going on in my own heart rather than what is happening on the outside. In Jesus' name, Amen.

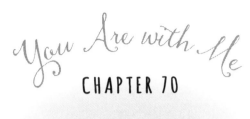

You Are with Me

CHAPTER 70

DO NOT FEAR

bravery, fear, going against the crowd

I kept having the same bad dream over and over again.

Standing in the hall of the junior high my siblings went to, I was in a sea of students, but felt all alone. Spinning my combination lock around and around, I couldn't stop at the right place. Seconds were slipping away. The bell would ring and I would still be standing, sweating in front of my locker.

Then, I would jolt awake, still in my bed. (You can see a picture of the house I grew up in on my scrapbook at LynnCowell. com. Just click on "books" and then *Brave Beauty*.)

What was wrong with me? Why was I so scared? What would my mom think if I told her? Would she understand what was going on in me?

I began to pray often about this fear of moving from elementary school to junior high school. I knew God could help me, I just didn't know what His help would look like.

Proverbs 3:25–26 (NIV) tells us "Have no fear of sudden disaster or of the ruin that overtakes the wicked, for the LORD will be at your side and will keep your foot from being snared."

God promises us He will be right at our side. Not in front of us so we feel like we have to try to catch up. Not behind us, making us go first. He is right next to us, close. He helps us not get tripped up along the way.

When we take our fears to God, we can confidently ask Him to help us through the scary thing we face. His help may be giving us confidence to move forward. His help may also mean changing some things so that we don't have to go through it at all.

For me, the way God came beside me was making a way for me to not go to the big junior high. The brave thing for me was to ask my parents if I could make a switch and attend a small school. They said "yes."

Our piece of the puzzle is to trust God and be on the lookout for Him to answer. His piece is to show us the way.

GETTING TO KNOW YOU

(Circle one answer below each question.)

How do you usually feel about change?

a. I like new things.

b. I never like new things.

c. Sometimes I do; sometimes I don't. It depends on what the change is.

When you need to do something new, do you prefer:

a. To have a friend do it with you.

b. Figure it out on your own.

c. Get advice from an adult before you do the new thing.

You mostly like new:

a. Foods.

b. Places to visit.

c. People.

COURAGEOUS CALL

Dear Father, thank you for hearing me when I call. Thank you for always being at my side. In Jesus' name, Amen.

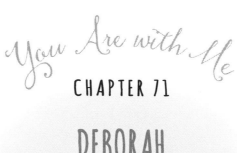

CHAPTER 71

DEBORAH

bravery, fear, going against the crowd

What would you think if God told you, "You are going to be a commander of an army of 10,000 men as they head into war?"

Woah—wait up a minute! I would think.

That is exactly what He told Deborah. Her story is found in Judges 4. Deborah was a prophet and the only female judge mentioned in the Bible. As a spokesperson to God's people, God gave her a message for a man named Barak: ". . . The LORD, the God of Israel, commands you: 'Go, take with you ten thousand men of Naphtali and Zebulun and lead them up to Mount Tabor." Judges 4:6b (NIV) God promised that when Barak obeyed him, God would take care of the rest and make sure they won the battle.

Barak responded to Deborah: "If you go with me, I will go; but if you don't go with me, I won't go." Judges 4:8 (NLT)

Go with you? Deborah might have thought she was only

God's messenger, but now it appeared she would be God's commander too.

In her time and culture, a female judge and war commander was not normal. Women didn't have these types of jobs. Ever.

Deborah knew God was with her. He had made that clear: "I will lead Sisera, the commander of Jabin's army, with his chariots and his troops to the Kishon River and give him into your hands.'" Judges 4:7 (NIV) Because God was with her, Deborah could confidently do what no woman had ever done.

What did God see in Deborah that made Him choose her, when all of his other judges were men? Why would God choose a woman to co-lead 10,000 men into war? Could God have possibly chosen her *because* she was so unlikely? Would the whole purpose of Him choosing her be to show how great He is?

I think so, and I think Deborah knew so. After the battle, when they had won, the Bible says, "On that day God subdued Jabin king of Canaan before the Israelites." Judges 4:23 (NIV). Whose name is missing here?

Deborah's. Barak's too. Only God's. God knew Deborah would point to God when it was all over.

Confident girls don't need the spotlight. They already have light in them; they don't need it on them. For this reason, when it comes to giving the attention and limelight to another, they are ok with that. For sure Deborah was and God received all the glory.

BECOMING BRAVE

How do you feel when you do something great, but another person gets the attention? What does your reaction say about the girl you are or about the girl you want to become?

_____

_____

_____

_____

COURAGEOUS CALL

Dear Lord, Deborah is one woman I want to be like. Unafraid. Fearless. Confident. No matter what You ask me to do, help me to confidently say "yes." In Jesus' name, Amen.

You Are with Me

CHAPTER 72

HE CAN DO IT

bravery, fear, going against the crowd

Chloe had been studying and studying for her math test. Every time she took a practice test, she failed. Overwhelmed and discouraged, she wanted to give up. She didn't though. Even if it seemed like she would never get it; she didn't quit. She asked her parents to pray for her. She had done her part; studying until she could study no more. Yet, even when she took her last practice test the morning of the actual test, she didn't pass. Now it was time for the real thing. She gave it her all and she got . . . drum roll please . . . She got a B!

After her test, Chloe was so happy. She came home from school so excited she could dance. She told her parents, "Thank you so much for praying for me!"

Chloe had felt discouraged, overwhelmed, and anxious. She knew that God was with her and within her, yet it didn't change how she felt. She said to her parents before she took the test, "The worst that can happen is I fail. Even if I do, I did my best and that is all I can do." When she went in to face her greatest fear, which would be failing the test, she knew that God was with her no matter what the outcome.

Chloe could trust in two things: she was ready to do her best and God was with her, this was the truth regardless of her anxious feelings.

The way God helped her that day was by helping her pass. Chloe acknowledged that God had helped her.

She found this verse to be true: ". . . I call on the LORD in my distress, and he answers me." Psalm 120:1 (NLT)

BECOMING BRAVE

Ask an adult in your life: "When was a time in your life that God answered your prayer in a way you didn't expect?" Hearing other people's story can build your faith for seeing God answer your own prayers.

COURAGEOUS CALL

Dear Lord, I know that You don't always answer my prayers the way I want or the way that I expect. But that never changes the fact that You are with me. That will never change because you never change. In Jesus' name, Amen.

CHAPTER 73

A HAIRY SITUATION

bravery, fear, going against the crowd

Mackenzie loved baking, especially birthday cakes. There was just something about making a sweet treat to surprise someone she loved. Pulling out all of the ingredients and setting up her perfect baking environment, the last thing to come out on the counter was the mixer.

First, Mackenzie mixed together the flour, cocoa powder, baking powder, and baking soda. Next she beat the butter, eggs, and vanilla. Gradually, she added sugar and turned the beater up from medium to high. Wait! What was happening? When she had leaned over, Mackenzie's long hair had gotten caught in the beaters and now the powerful machine was pulling her hair out. Before she could turn the mixer off, a chunk of her beautiful, long hair was gone.

As if this wasn't bad enough, Mackenzie had an orchestra concert the next week. As a violinist, she was in the front row.

When she asked her conductor if she could wear a cap for the concert, she was told no. "That wouldn't be appropriate" her conductor had said.

Mackenzie was caught in a tough situation. She could not go to the concert. If she didn't, she would not have to deal with being embarrassed, but she would suffer by missing the concert. Mackenzie could also go for it and trust that God would help her get past her awkwardness.

What would you do?

Mackenzie did it; she went to the concert and played her part. This courageous step was the beginning of knowing that who she is isn't based on how she looks.

Habakkuk 3:19 (NIV) encourages us, "God, the LORD, is my strength; he makes my feet like the deer's; he makes me tread on my high places . . ."

The Lord is my strength. You've been reading that throughout this whole book. But what is this part about comparing our feet to that of a deer? That is such a strange comparison!

We have a family of deer that live in our front yard. Day and night, they eat, sleep, and romp around our yard. Sometimes, they leap down from our stone wall with no effort at all.

Deer have feet called hooves. These hooves help them to not fall when they run down something slippery like a steep mountainside, by digging into the soil.

God is saying to you and me, that when we're in slippery situations, He will not let us fall. Like Mackenzie with her bald spot and orchestra concert, when you are in a slippery spot, He will be your strength to do the hard thing. He will give you the courage you need to not fall.

BECOMING BRAVE

Look up a picture of a deer's hoof and see what makes their feet so different from ours. In what ways, other than our feet, has God made us different from animals?

_____

_____

_____

_____

COURAGEOUS CALL

Dear Lord, it is so amazing how You gave every part of creation exactly what they need for where they live. Help me to trust that You will give me everything I need for the way you want me to live. In Jesus' name, Amen.

CHAPTER 74

A VIDEO FOR CHANGE

bullying, friendship, loving others, bravery, courage

Alivia had been bullied in fifth grade, and now it was happening to other people. Alivia kept feeling that she needed to **do** something for kids who were bullied to let them know that they were not alone. This thought was always on her mind, festering like a sore that needed medical help.

Finally, the idea came—she could make a video. She could use her creativity to make a video that would encourage kids who were being bullied and help them to know they were not alone.

You can see the video Alivia made here: https://www.youtube.com/watch?time_continue=11&v=KwQTuTyqZ_M

Bullying has become all too common. In the classroom, words are exchanged that hurt. On social media, kids feel comfortable saying things they would never say face-to-face. Bullying can empower a girl to feel a corrupt confidence that comes from two different places. This bullying bravery can come from arrogance; an exaggerated self-opinion that makes her believe she is better than others. And strangely enough, this confidence also comes from feeling insecure. Uncertain and uncomfortable with herself, she somehow believes that if she can make another girl look "less-than" it will make her look better.

In Matthew 22:39 (NIV) Jesus says, "And a second [commandment] is like it: You shall love your neighbor as yourself."

The girl who bullies because she thinks she is better than others is not following Jesus' command—He tells us to love others. The girl who bullies because she is insecure is not following Jesus' command either. She is not loving others and she is not loving herself either.

Understanding why people bully others can help us bring this craze to an end. You can fear others less and be brave enough to stop and stand up. You can be the change!

GETTING TO KNOW YOU

(*Circle one answer below each question.*)

When you feel that others are putting you down, you usually:

a. Look for a place to hide.

b. Ignore them.

c. Stand up for yourself.

How common is bullying at your school, on the field, or on the computer?

a. I see it all the time.

b. It is pretty rare.

c. I know it is out there, but I'm not around people who act that way.

Have you been a victim of bullying?

a. Yes, many times.

b. I've been teased, but I brushed it off and tried to move on.

c. No, I haven't.

COURAGEOUS CALL

Dear Father, bullying breaks Your heart. Help me stop before I say hurtful words. Help me see when others are hurting people. Give me wisdom to know what to say and do to see bullying come to an end. In Jesus' name, Amen.

CHAPTER 75

HER TURN

bravery, fear, going against the crowd

Do you like a story with a beautiful heroine, a villain, suspense, and a happy ending? Then you *have* to read the book of Esther.

Esther, a Jewish orphan, grew up in Persia as a captive. The king of Persia was looking for a new queen, so he appointed officers to go throughout his country, looking for "beautiful young virgins" Esther 2:2 (NIV). These girls were brought to the palace where they spent a year doing all they could to enhance their beauty. Esther was one of these girls.

After one year, the king chose Esther as his queen.

Now there was a man in the king's court named Haman who wanted to be famous. He hated Esther's people, the Jews. He believed they stood in the way of his goals. He created a sinister plot to have them killed. The king gave Haman permission to carry out his plan. What Haman and the king didn't know was that Queen Esther was Jewish!

Esther's cousin Mordecai told her of Haman's terrible plot to kill the Jews. He challenged Esther, saying the reason she was queen was so she could save her people.

Esther had a choice. She could not say a word, hoping no one would find out she was Jewish and live. Or she could choose to be brave, risking her own life to save her people.

There was a rule in the land that if you wanted to speak to the king, he had to ask you to come to his throne; you could never ask him. If you did, you were put to death! Esther asked all of her people to fast with her for three days. Then, she would plead with the king to save her people.

Esther prepared a huge feast and invited the king to come to the feast. He said yes. While eating and drinking, Esther told the king of Haman's horrible plan. The king was furious! Instead of Esther's people being killed, the king had Haman killed. Esther's courage saved not only herself, but her entire nation.

Maybe God has you at the school you attend, the church you are a part of, the team you play on, or the neighborhood you live in so that He can use you right there—right now. You see something that is unfair or not right. God can use you to bring change. Will you stay comfortable or will you take the risk and trust God to use you?

BECOMING BRAVE

Become an investigator. Learn about what you see that is not right in your world. What can you do, no matter how small, to help bring change?

COURAGEOUS CALL

Dear God, I want to make a difference. May I be fearless in bringing change to my world. In Jesus' name, Amen.

I Can Stand Up for Others

CHAPTER 76

I WOULDN'T SAY THAT

bravery, fear, going against the crowd

Ashley loved showing horses, but competition between the girls could be fierce. At the horse shows, each rider does her very best to show off her greatest skill. With every girl trying her hardest and being judged for their performance, it's the perfect scenario for the riders to not just be judged by the judges, but to judge each other.

After one particular show, one of Ashley's riding friends made fun of another rider. Ashley stood up to the rider who spoke the mean comments, letting her know it wasn't nice. They were all doing their best, weren't they? The funny thing is, the girl she was making fun of ended up winning the show!

Proverbs 31:8a (NIV) encourages us, "Speak up for those who cannot speak for themselves . . ." In this case, the other rider couldn't speak up for herself because she wasn't a part of the conversation. Ashley stood up for her friend.

The thing about mean girl conversations is that what we say

so often comes back to us. "Do not be deceived: God cannot be mocked. A man reaps what he sows" says Galatians 6:7 (NIV). This means that what we give out we will get back. If we speak mean words, mean words will be spoken of us. The great thing is that the reverse is also true! When we choose kind words, one day kind words will be said of us as well.

The verse from Galatians 6:7 comes from the world of farming. The people Paul was writing to would have been familiar with planting seeds, watching them grow, and then reaping or harvesting what was planted.

Today, many of us plant gardens like those in the past. Gardening can be fun and rewarding. My girls and I plant flowers in our backyard and enjoy seeing the gorgeous flowers bloom. What we sow we reap in beautiful blooms.

That is exactly what the Lord wants for us. He wants us to sow seeds of kindness and love so those things will come back to us.

BECOMING BRAVE

Plan some time for planting. Create a plan for what and where you can plant vegetables or flowers. Get books from the library and learn what climate zone you live in. This will tell you what plants grow best in your area and when is the best time to plant. Gardening might become your new hobby.

COURAGEOUS CALL

Dear Lord, help me remember that the words I say are not random. They are seeds I sow. What I say will come back to me one day. Help me to be confident in You and not afraid to speak up for those who cannot speak up for themselves. In Jesus' name, Amen.

CHAPTER 77

WILL YOU BE MY FRIEND?

bravery, fear, going against the crowd

Every day, Chad looked for someone to talk to at lunch. Most of the kids had a group or at least a certain friend that they liked to sit with each day. Not Chad. His learning needs meant that he was not in the same classroom as many of the other kids. Playing the games they played during break was hard for him; he often didn't understand the rules. His struggle to fit in made him that much more awkward. It's not that the kids were mean—they simply ignored him.

Then Chad met Dominque. When he approached her in the lunch room, she smiled at him. He asked her if he could sit by her and she warmly said yes. She didn't ignore his questions, in fact, she asked him questions back. Chad felt like he had found a friend in Dominque.

Dominque might not have known it, but she was following God's instructions in Proverbs 31:8–9 (NIV) "Speak up for those who cannot speak for themselves, for the rights of all who are destitute. Speak up and judge fairly; defend the rights of the poor and needy."

Chad was needy; he needed a friend.

It can be hard to be a friend to those who really need friends. There are some who will put you down or make fun of you for reaching out to those who are different than you. Those who make fun of others do not have a right way of looking at themselves. They may either think they are better than others or they may think so little of themselves that putting others down makes them feel better.

The confident girl cares more about being kind than she cares about what others will think or say about her. She knows she is most like Jesus when she loves others.

BECOMING BRAVE

What can you do today to speak up for someone who cannot speak up for themselves? Maybe there is someone in your class who struggles with being shy or a student who needs a little extra help with their work. Like an investigator, be on the lookout for someone who needs you. Step up and be their help today.

COURAGEOUS CALL

Dear Jesus, I want to be so confident in the girl You made me that I don't have to always think about my needs. I want to think of others and what they need and then find a way to meet them. In Jesus' name, Amen.

I Can Overcome

CHAPTER 78

MOVING FORWARD

overcoming fear, physical problems, fear of people, courage, strength, confidence

Riding horses made Ashley feel free. There was nothing she loved more than getting on the back of a horse and riding.

One thing about horses, though. They are animals and they can be unpredictable.

One day, Ashley was having a great ride. She had jumped over four jumps on her horse, Moe. Right before the fifth jump, Moe stopped. He suddenly turned left, flinging Ashley over the top of him and slamming her into the jump.

Ashley laid on the ground. Did she break something? All she knew was she hurt all over. After a while she got up. She was ready to go home.

That is not what her trainer had in mind. She pushed Ashley to get back on the horse right then and there. She had to try it again, her trainer said. If she didn't, Ashley would be even more fearful the next time she came to ride. Encouraging her every step of the way, her trainer helped Ashley as she faced her fears and got back on Moe.

Today, Ashley is not afraid of horses or of jumping. She faced "the worst that could happen" and it turned out well.

It can be hard to understand why bad things happen. Why did Moe throw Ashley? We don't know, but we do know that hard times can make us stronger girls.

James 1:2–4 (NIV) tells us, "Consider it pure joy, my brothers and sisters, whenever you face trials of many kinds, because you know that the testing of your faith produces perseverance. Let perseverance finish its work so that you may be mature and complete, not lacking anything." Getting back up and doing it again developed perseverance in Ashley. She learned that even when things don't go right, she can get up and try again. This test helped her to move forward, toward becoming a mature girl.

Chances are you will not be thrown from a horse, but you will definitely experience difficulties. It takes a brave girl to see those difficulties as a chance to grow. That is what you are—brave and beautiful!

BECOMING BRAVE

Ask someone you respect to tell you of a time that she experienced a trial or something that felt like a failure and how it helped her become more mature.

COURAGEOUS CALL

Dear Lord, falling off a horse? That is not fun! It sounds like growing more mature can be painful. I don't want to be a little child all my life, though. I want to grow up to be strong, brave, and confident. When the hard times come, help me to remember that trials are meant to help me grow. In Jesus' name, Amen.

CHAPTER 79

A BIG JOB TO DO

overcoming fear, physical problems, fear of people, courage, strength, confidence

God had a big job that needed to be done and He knew just the guy to do it. The Israelites had been slaves for over 400 years. They cried out to God for help. God heard their cries and was ready to put Moses in place.

One day while Moses was out watching sheep, a miracle happened. "There the angel of the LORD appeared to him in a blazing fire from the middle of a bush. Moses stared in amazement. Though the bush was engulfed in flames, it didn't burn up. "This is amazing," Moses said to himself. "Why isn't that bush burning up? I must go see it." Exodus 3:2–3 (NLT)

As Moses drew closer to the bush, God spoke, "Look! The cry of the people of Israel has reached me, and I have seen how harshly the Egyptians abuse them. Now go, for I am sending you to Pharaoh. You must lead my people Israel out of Egypt." (v. 9–10)

The first thing out of Moses' mouth revealed his fear and lack of self-esteem, ". . . Who am I to appear before Pharaoh? Who am I to lead the people of Israel out of Egypt?" God answered, "I will be with you . . ." (v.11b–12a)

God says He will be with Moses, but Moses felt that wasn't enough. He kept telling God reasons why he couldn't do what God was calling him to do. Then Moses revealed his insecurity, ". . . LORD, I'm not very good with words. I never have been, and I'm not now, even though you have spoken to me. I get tongue-tied, and my words get tangled." Exodus 4:10 (NLT)

Moses' confidence is choking on the words he can't seem to get out. He is so wrapped up in his problem, he can't hear Almighty God say *He* is with Moses. God promises Moses that He will perform miracles through him and do everything Moses needs, but Moses just can't get past what he hears when he talks— his own voice.

Friend, whatever keeps you from being confident, God has the solution for you! Just as He was with Moses, He is with you. You may not be facing down a king, but God is still backing you up. Like Moses, He may send someone to come alongside you. Like Moses, He may give you abilities you never had before. One thing we know for sure, He will be with you!

BECOMING BRAVE

Moses allowed his speech impediment to keep him from becoming confident. Is there something in your life you need to overcome? Eventually Moses went and spoke to Pharaoh. Draw a picture below of you taking steps to overcome your confidence drainer.

COURAGEOUS CALL

Dear Jesus, the thought of overcoming my fear both terrifies me and excites me. Help me to think of myself, picture myself, as one who is confident. In Jesus' name, Amen.

I Can Overcome

CHAPTER 80

TELL SOMEONE

overcoming fear, physical problems, fear of people, courage, strength, confidence, fear

Allie's parents had an anniversary coming up so they planned to take a trip for just the two of them. They asked a family member they trusted to come and stay with their children while they were away.

During the trip, Allie's caretaker hurt her. Allie wasn't sure what to do. Should she tell her parents? If she did tell them, should she wait until her parents got back or should she call them on their trip? She didn't want to interrupt their vacation, but she thought this was important.

Being 10 years old was hard. Since Allie was young, would people believe her?

Though it took so much bravery, Allie called her mom and

told her what happened. Her parents came home as fast as they could.

Having someone she trusted hurt her was very hard on Allie. This person was someone who was supposed to love her and take care of her; not hurt her.

After Allie's parents came home, there were many times Allie had to be brave. She had to be brave when she told the police. And she had to have courage when she met with a social worker who could help her understand what happened and help her to heal from the hurt.

But of all of those times, the hardest was that very first step—choosing to tell her mom. Allie believed that if she told her mom she would believe Allie and help her. Allie was right. It was the best thing she could have done.

Allie could not understand why someone would choose to hurt her. But even though she could not understand, she didn't want helplessness or hopelessness stuck in her heart. She chose to trust her mom to get her the help she needed. And she accepted the help her mom found.

Jesus says in John 15:12 (ESV), "This is my commandment, that you love one another as I have loved you." That is what Allie's mom did. By believing Allie and getting her the help she needed, she loved Allie like Jesus loves Allie.

If you are in a situation where someone is hurting you or someday you find yourself in that place, it will take bravery to tell someone you need help. Know this—it is the very best thing you can do to help yourself.

BECOMING BRAVE

Share Allie's story with your parent or an adult you trust. If you or someone you know is in a situation like Allie was, bravely tell this adult and ask them to help.

COURAGEOUS CALL

Dear Jesus, it doesn't seem right that big people hurt little people sometimes. If I am ever in this situation, give me strength and wisdom to do what I need to do to get help. In Jesus' name, Amen.

CHAPTER 81

YOU CAN OVERCOME ANYTHING

*overcoming fear, physical problems, fear of
people, courage, strength, confidence*

"What happened to your leg?" is a question my friend Mandy is asked every day.

From the time Mandy was nine months old, her body has struggled with many life threatening infections causing her to be hospitalized over 100 times. Trying to stop one of these infections from spreading and to save her life, doctors amputated Mandy's leg and hip when she was eight years old. But this surgery didn't stop the illness.

For years her family traveled all over the country begging doctors to find out why Mandy continued to get life threatening infections. She's had hundreds and perhaps thousands of tests done on her body and blood. For you and me, waiting days or a week for a doctor to explain why we are sick can be almost unbearable. Mandy's family waited twenty-three years to figure out what was wrong.

Here is what Mandy says about all of the troubles she has had to overcome and continues to overcome every day:

"I know I've had this disease for a reason; it's not for my purpose, but for Jesus'. My life is not about me. Unlike what my generation wants us to believe, it's about Him! Knowing that He is in charge of my life gives me hope for those things that seem so unclear, like my disease and living without answers for so many years. I don't blame God nor am I angry with God for all that has happened to me. Actually, as crazy as this may sound, I thank God for choosing me."

Choosing me? Why does Mandy say "choosing me"? Because now, Mandy travels speaking to girls of all ages, sharing with them how much Jesus loves them and says that they are beautiful just the way they are . . . no matter what others see on the outside.

Mandy loves to share 1 Chronicles 16:8 (NIV), "Give thanks to the LORD and proclaim his greatness. Let the whole world know what he has done." This is exactly what Mandy does as she shares with other people the strength she has found in Jesus to go through all of her troubles.

Your troubles may not be as big as Mandy's, but no matter what hard things you face each day, God can help you to keep going. Like He has with Mandy, He can make your life a story that you can share with others as you share his greatness in you.

BECOMING BRAVE

Mandy likes to design T-shirts that have positive messages on them to encourage girls in their faith. Design your own T-shirt with a message that would help girls become brave. Draw it below.

COURAGEOUS CALL

Dear Jesus, thank you for Mandy and others like her who are brave. Help me know that with You, I can face anything that comes in this life. In Jesus' name, Amen.

CHAPTER 82

TWO ARE BETTER THAN ONE

encourage others, friendships

Having just finished a seminar on bullying, Shannon knew she needed to be part of the solution. What could she do? She began to think as well as ask family and friends what ideas they might have.

Shannon decided to start a club at her school called **Bully Busters**. She would encourage the kids in her school to come together to stop bullying. When they would see another student being put down or picked on, they would kindly bring it to a stop by sticking together.

As Shannon began to share her idea, at first others thought her idea was strange. Shannon tried not to become discouraged and hoped her idea would catch on.

When we are brave, we pave the way for others to be brave. A famous preacher named Billy Graham said, "Courage is contagious. When a brave man takes a stand, the spines of others are often stiffened." (https://www.brainyquote.com/quotes/quotes/b/billygraha113622.html)

When we are brave together, we become stronger. Ecclesiastes 4:9 (NIV) says, "Two are better than one, because they have a good return for their labor:" Two or more people, joined together, are able to do so much more than one can do alone. Fear fades away when we do something scary together.

GETTING TO KNOW YOU

(Circle one answer below each question.)

Have you ever made fun of someone?

a. Yes, but I wish I hadn't.

b. Yes, but I've never really thought of that as bullying someone.

c. No, I never want to see someone hurt.

Where do you see bullying happening the most?

a. In the lunch room.

b. During break time.

c. On social media.

If you have ever been made fun of, did you:

a. Let it bother you for a really long time.

b. Get over it quickly.

c. Realize the person hurting others was the person hurting inside.

COURAGEOUS CALL

Dear Jesus, I want to be a bully buster too. Help me to stick up for others in small ways and in big ways! In Jesus' name, Amen.

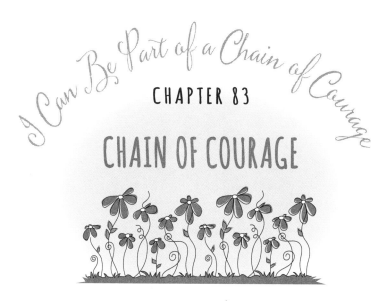

CHAPTER 83

CHAIN OF COURAGE

encourage others, friendship

If the story in Exodus 1:15–Exodus 2:10 were a play, it could be called *A Chain of Courage*. It might look like this:

Act 1: Shiphrah and Puah, women who help deliver babies in Egypt, are commanded by Pharaoh to kill all male babies when they are born. The brave women obey God rather than Pharaoh.

Act 2: Shiphrah, Puah, and Jochebed, Moses' mother, in between Jochebed's labor pains, discuss what they should do if her child is a boy. How would Jochebed answer questions about her delivery? Where could they put the baby as he grew? How long could they keep him a secret? Whispering, they create a plan.

As they plan, they talk about their history with God. He had proven that He could and would care for them, even in this foreign country. As they created these God-inspired plans, their confidence in God grows and their fears weaken. Cowardice gives way to courage when we remember what God has done for us.

Once Moses is born, Jochebed courageously hides him at

home. When she can no longer keep him a secret, she puts her baby in a basket, hiding him in the Nile River.

Act 3: Miriam, Moses' sister, stands by, watching the basket float on the Nile. But she isn't just observing. When Pharaoh's daughter calls for the basket to be brought to her, Miriam steps up, giving the princess advice on how the child can be cared for.

Do you see the chain effect one woman's courage has on another?

Shiphrah and Puah decided to go against Pharaoh.

Jochebed saw their courage and decided to bravely hide Moses. Miriam, seeing her mother's courage, fearlessly approaches Pharaoh's daughter.

A ripple effect can take place when one person takes a daring step and others see it. News of Shiphrah and Puah disobeying the Pharaoh's horrible command would have traveled through their community, reaching Jochebed. Miriam would have watched her mother's fearlessness as she took care of Moses. Miriam confidently approached the princess.

You can be part of a chain of courage too! When you step up and are brave, others will see, and your actions may help them to be brave too.

BECOMING BRAVE

Let's make a chain of paper to decorate your room.

Take a piece of pretty scrapbooking or construction paper and cut it into strips. Make the first link by bending the paper and connecting the two ends with tape, glue, or staples. Add another link by threading another strip through the center of the first loop. Connect the ends together. Keep adding links.

On each link, write the name of someone you know, or from history, who has been brave. As you learn of more brave people, add their names.

COURAGEOUS CALL

Dear Jesus, help me to become a link in a chain of courage. In Jesus' name, Amen.

CHAPTER 84

THE RIPPLE EFFECT

encourage others, friendship

When Allie was ten years old, someone she trusted hurt her. Telling an adult and then taking the steps to heal from that hurt was very hard on Allie. This person was someone who was supposed to love her and take care of her, not hurt her.

The brave steps Allie took developed a confidence in her that was sure and strong.

Not only did Allie learn that there are trustworthy adults she can go to when she needs help, she also learned God would never let her down. This painful process was a challenging way to become confident, but even at her young age, she took the worst and worked to put her faith in God instead of becoming fainthearted.

Because someone stuck up for Allie and helped her, Allie knew she needed to stick up for a friend who was in a desperate situation. Allie approached this friend, offering to come alongside her, but her friend didn't want that. Telling another person scared her.

266

Allie knew the courage it would take and she knew her friend didn't have it at that moment. But Allie had courage **for** her friend. She went to the school social worker and shared with this trusted adult what was happening in her friend's life. She knew there are courageous, trustworthy adults who are trained to help people who are hurting and don't know where to turn. She knew because she had been helped by them herself.

Being brave can have a ripple effect—it makes a difference not just in your life, but in other's as well. We can be the beginning of that ripple effect. Ecclesiastes 4:9–12 (NIV) tells us, "Two are better than one, because they have a good return for their labor: If either of them falls down, one can help the other up. But pity anyone who falls and has no one to help them up.

Also, if two lie down together, they will keep warm. But how can one keep warm alone?

Though one may be overpowered, two can defend themselves. A cord of three strands is not quickly broken." We need each other to become brave!

After Allie shared with the social worker, her friend got the help she needed. Her friend had fallen down, but because of Allie's actions to help her up, she began the road to recovery.

BECOMING BRAVE

Do you know adults that you could turn to or help a friend go to if you needed help?

COURAGEOUS CALL

Dear Lord, I want to be the type of friend that Allie is. I want to be the first in a ripple effect of fearless actions. The only way I can do that, Lord, is if your Holy Spirit does it through me. In Jesus' name, Amen.

I Can Be Part of a Chain of Courage

CHAPTER 85

FRIENDS PULL YOU THROUGH

encourage others, friendship

I woke up this morning feeling afraid. You know, we can't control what we feel. Feelings are just like that sometimes. Encouragement or discouragement. Fearlessness or fearfulness. They can just come over us.

It's what we **do** with those feelings that makes all the difference.

We can allow the negative feelings to stay. We can keep thinking about that thing we're scared of. Like me, finishing writing this book. I felt scared. *Will they like it? Will they think my writing is good? Will I get it done on time?*

These thoughts tried to grow from feelings to fear.

So, I asked for my friends to pray for me.

I put on my Facebook page: "I know God has given me this assignment and I don't want to be fearful. I don't want to give in to pressure that I know doesn't come from Him." As I shared my need for prayer and strength, my friends prayed for me. I became strong from their prayers.

It was a chain effect.

I was brave, sharing my feelings with my friends. My friends used their strength to pray for me. God heard and helped me be strong and do what God had given me to do.

Maybe you have been told to "follow your heart." Jeremiah 17:9 tells us that we can't follow our heart because our heart will lie to us. My heart tried to lie to me this morning, telling me to be afraid when there was no reason to be afraid. God is with me!

We can't control our feelings, but we can learn to control our response to those feelings. My friend Renee Swope says we need to boss our feelings around; not let them boss us around. The more we choose to not allow our feelings to boss us around, the more our confidence will grow. We will see that our feelings don't have to control us. With God's power in us, we can learn to boss our feelings around more and more. Confidence will come when we see what He will do in us and what we can do in Him.

BECOMING BRAVE

Over the next couple of hours, pay attention to your feelings. Write down your feelings here.

Of these feelings, which ones did you like? Which ones didn't you like?

Of the feelings you didn't like, what could you tell yourself that is positive that would turn those feelings around?

_____

_____

_____

_____

COURAGEOUS CALL

Dear Jesus, my feelings are powerful. I can go from laughing to crying so quickly! I like the idea of knowing that I don't have to let my feelings push me around. You can and will help me switch my feelings from negative to positive and become a confident girl if I will only learn to trust You. In Jesus' name, Amen.

CHAPTER 86

NO ONE GETS ME

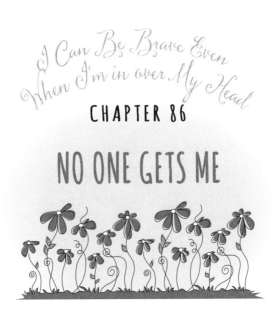

overwhelmed, scared

When Katie's parents told her they were getting a divorce, she wasn't surprised. She *was* sad. Her sadness was so deep and strong she couldn't even talk about it. She didn't want to tell her friends. She didn't want to talk to her grandparents. Her heart just ached.

Then things went from hard to horrible. She heard her parents talking on the phone about whom she would live with and when she would live there.

Katie didn't want to move from house to house. She wanted to live in **her** house all the time . . . with both of her parents. Didn't they get that? Wasn't what she needed enough to make her parents work out their trouble? When she was brave and shared her feelings with her parents, they became angry with her. "You're too young to understand," they said. Maybe she was young, but she wanted them to understand her just like they wanted her to understand them.

Sometimes we'll have feelings and fears others won't understand. Often they can't because they are not you. Feeling misunderstood can make us feel less confident. *Is there something wrong with me?*

When we don't feel understood, we can feel alone. God tells us then, even when others don't get us, He will. He made us, so we aren't weird or quirky to Him. We're just like He made us to be.

I love the reassurance David felt from the Lord. He wrote in Psalm 139:1 (NIV): "You have searched me, Lord, and you know me." That sentence makes me want to take a deep breath and sigh. Ahhhhhh . . . Even if my family doesn't get me, even if my closest friend misunderstands me, God gets me.

Friend, even if no one understands you, God does. You can tell Him your frustrations, fears, and feelings. He will understand. He won't get mad, judge, or think the worst of you.

Knowing God gets me gives me confidence. I can move forward and keep on growing because He is in me and helps me. He is in you and helping you too!

GETTING TO KNOW YOU

(*Circle one answer below each question.*)

Who do you feel understands you the most?

a. Your parent.

b. Your best friend.

c. Your sibling.

When I feel misunderstood, I usually:

a. Try to be alone.

b. Keep talking, hoping the other person will eventually understand.

c. Give up and talk about something else.

Does knowing God understands you make you feel:

a. Peaceful.

b. Confident.

c. Comforted.

COURAGEOUS CALL

Dear God, knowing You understand me helps me to not feel so alone. I know that no one can get inside of my head and get all of me, except You who created me. Thank you so much for Your friendship, God. I love you. In Jesus' name, Amen.

I Can Be Brave Even When I'm in over My Head

CHAPTER 87

MIRIAM THE MOVER

overwhelmed, scared

Being the oldest child can bring with it all kinds of responsibilities; one of them being taking care of younger siblings.

In the book of Exodus Miriam was the oldest sister to Aaron and Moses. They lived at a time when the people of Israel were slaves in Egypt. Pharaoh was nervous because the Israelite tribe kept increasing as God blessed them more and more. As a result of his fear, he made a decree: every newborn boy was to be killed.

Miriam's mother saved her son, Moses, by putting him in a basket in the river.

I wonder what Miriam was thinking as she watched her mom create the basket and prepare to put her brother in it. *Will this hold him up, Lord? What if a crocodile gets him?* (At one point in time, sixteen feet long 1,500 pound crocodiles lived in the Nile River! That alone would be enough to terrify me!)

Miriam went down to the water to watch her brother.

Nothing in the Bible tells us that Miriam went down to the water because her mom told her to. Miriam did what she believed was right. It was as if she already knew what Paul would write one day, "Don't let anyone look down on you because you are young, but set an example for the believers in speech, in conduct, in love, in faith and in purity." 1 Timothy 4:12 (NIV)

Miriam was not only brave enough to go down to this river loaded with reptiles, she spoke to the princess when her brother was discovered. Then, this gutsy girl went on to offer her advice! As Paul said, she didn't look down on herself because she was young and she didn't expect a princess to look down on her either.

Miriam not only stood by her brother that time, but she also came alongside Moses later in his life when God used him to move their people out of slavery. Using her gifts of music and poetry, Miriam helped God's people worship Him while they were moving through the desert.

Although Miriam was an ordinary child, she grew up to become an extraordinary adult.

BECOMING BRAVE

Have you ever ridden in boat or gone swimming in a river, lake, or ocean? How is swimming in a natural area that might have animals in it different from swimming in a swimming pool? Do you think you have to be brave to do this?

COURAGEOUS CALL

Dear God, as I grow older, I want to grow braver, like Miriam. Use me to make a difference in my world. In Jesus' name, Amen.

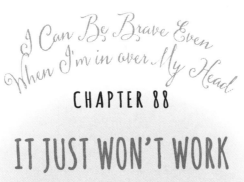

I Can Be Brave Even
When I'm in over My Head

CHAPTER 88

IT JUST WON'T WORK

overwhelmed, scared

The science fair was only two weeks away and I still had no idea what I was going to do for a project.

My friends seemed to all have great ideas. Some of their ideas sounded so complicated, I wondered if their parents had done them.

My growing fear of failure fueled my procrastination. I was in over my head.

Finally, a week before it was due, I found a project I liked. I would demonstrate how the stem of a plant delivers what the plant needs to grow.

One area in my life where I have always had to grow is in following directions. Even if I take the time to read the directions, I often read them too fast and don't pay attention to the details.

In this case I skimmed the instructions for this science project, then asked my mom to purchase a white carnation and food coloring. I then filled a glass with water, put two drops of red in the glass, stuck my flower in the water, and went to bed. I couldn't wait to wake up to a pink carnation.

The next morning, the carnation was as white as it was when I went to bed. *I just knew it! I am no good in science,* I thought.

The night before I had felt so confident; now I just felt like a failure. I wanted to quit.

In Paul's letter to the Hebrews, he gave them this advice: "So do not throw away your confidence; it will be richly rewarded." Hebrews 10:35 (NIV)

When we feel like we've failed, it is easy to throw away our confidence. We can give up, telling ourselves we don't have what it takes. Yet God has given us everything we need to succeed. Our part is to hang in there when we're in the middle of our mess.

I went back and read the directions again. I had missed many details that were key to my success. Once I began again and followed each step, my project succeeded. Just like Hebrews 10:35 said, ". . . it was richly rewarded."

BECOMING BRAVE

Try my science experiment for yourself.

Fill a glass ¼ full of water. Add 10 or more drops of food coloring. Trim the bottom of a white carnation, put it in the glass, and let it sit for a day.

The color of the flower changes because of what it takes in. We can make this comparison to what we take into our heart and mind. How are they impacted by what we take in through songs, movies, books, and videos?

COURAGEOUS CALL

Dear God, when things don't go my way, I can easily throw away my confidence. Before I begin beating myself up when things go wrong, help me to first determine not to throw away my confidence. In Jesus' name, Amen.

CHAPTER 89

POSITIVE THROUGH THE PAIN

overwhelmed, scared.

For as long as she could remember Hayley's hip made a loud popping sound when she walked. It didn't hurt for years, but as she grew and started playing sports, the popping *and* pain became worse.

Hayley needed to have hip surgery to correct the fact that her hip hadn't grown the way it should have. This surgery meant that Hayley had to use a wheelchair at school. When she was strong enough, she was able to use crutches.

This time was hard for Hayley; she felt out of control and in over her head. It also meant that there were many things Hayley couldn't do for herself like carrying her bag into school.

Hayley needed others to not only help her, but also to comfort her. Not being able to do so many of the things she was used to doing for herself made her very sad.

Even now, everything is not as it should be for Hayley. Every day she chooses to be brave as she faces another surgery and the rehabilitation that will follow to help her muscles become strong around her hip.

While so much is out of her control, Hayley has chosen to find the courage she needs in the Lord. She is confident He will heal her completely and help her through this time.

The Bible tells us in Isaiah 42:2 (NLT), "When you go through deep waters, I will be with you. When you go through rivers of difficulty, you will not drown. When you walk through the fire of oppression, you will not be burned up; the flames will not consume you."

Do you see that really important word—"when"? It doesn't say "if". God promises us that when we go through rivers of difficulty, we will not drown. He teaches us to swim in the waters of our troubles. When we learn His promises, they are the strength that holds us up and keeps us above water!

BECOMING BRAVE

When we are in a pool or the ocean and the water is over our head, we can either sink or swim. Before we can swim, though, we have to learn **how** to swim. If you know how to swim, think of the process you went through to learn. (If you don't remember what that looked like, ask your parent how you learned to swim.) How can you compare learning to swim to getting through hard times in life?

_____

_____

_____

_____

COURAGEOUS CALL

Dear God, it is best to learn how to swim before you're in deep water. Help me to practice depending on You now so that when I am in deep waters in my life, I won't be caught off guard. In Jesus' name, Amen.

CHAPTER 90

TALKING TO YOURSELF AGAIN

courage, self-talk, confidence

I've started this new habit in the past couple of months. I talk to myself. It might be a result of spending so much time alone now that my kids are in school. I don't really mind. I like listening to myself.

Actually, there is scientific research that tells us listening to ourselves can be good for us when we are saying good things about ourselves. When we talk to ourselves, whether the words we are saying are positive or negative, science tells us we believe ourselves!

As happens so often, what science has "discovered" God already revealed in the Bible.

In Deuteronomy 7, God is preparing his people, the Israelites, to move into a new land. The Israelites, who had been slaves in Egypt, began to doubt what they had the ability to do. Check out this verse in Deuteronomy 7:17 (NIV), "You may say to yourselves, "These nations are stronger than we are. How can we drive them out?"

God is the one who is speaking in this sentence. He is pointing out to His people that they may be tempted to speak negative words to themselves. In this case, those words are, "How are we going to do this?"

God goes on to tell them in verse 18, "But do not be afraid of them; remember well what the LORD your God did to Pharaoh and to all Egypt." Here God again says, "Do not be afraid." How will they go about not being afraid? They will not be afraid by remembering what God did for them before.

God instructs His people to review their history with Him. They are to go over in their minds all that He has done for them. When we remember what He has done for us, it builds us up to have faith in Him to do it again.

GETTING TO KNOW YOU

(Circle one answer below each question.)

Whether we realize it or not, we all talk to ourselves. When you talk to yourself, do you:

a. Talk to yourself only with thoughts in your mind.
b. Sometimes you talk to yourself out loud.
c. Both.

What kind of thoughts do you usually think about yourself?

a. Positive thoughts.
b. Negative thoughts.
c. I don't know; I'll start paying more attention.

When are you the most aware of what you are thinking?

a. When I first wake up in the morning.
b. When I am lying in bed at night.
c. When riding in the car.

COURAGEOUS CALL

Dear Lord, help me to stop any negative thoughts in my mind and begin to build up my confidence with positive thoughts about myself. In Jesus' name, Amen.

CHAPTER 91

TURN IT AROUND

courage, self-talk, confidence

"I am so bad at math! I should just give up. I'll never get this; I am so dumb." Monica was at it again. Calling herself names and saying negative things that make her feel even worse about her failing test grade in math. If only she could escape this subject and never have to face it again.

What Monica has gotten in the habit of doing is what my friend, Tracie Miles, calls "awfulizing." She applied that one defeat, her failed test grade, to her entire life. She wasn't just saying her test was a failure; she told herself *she* was a failure. As Tracie says, "We convince ourselves that if some things aren't good, nothing is good. If someone doesn't like us, nobody likes us. If a circumstance is hard, then our whole life is hard." (*Unsinkable Faith*, pg. 116)

We can too easily use powerful words in a negative way to describe ourselves and talk about our lives; words such as never, always, and forever. In reality, it is very hard to find anything in our lives that truly is never, always, and forever. It is not true that we never get it right, that we always mess up, or that we will forever struggle with this thing or that.

Words like never, always, and forever should be reserved only for describing God.

God will never leave us: "Be strong and courageous. Do not be afraid or terrified because of them, for the LORD your God goes with you; he will never leave you nor forsake you." Deuteronomy 31:6 (NIV).

God always leads us: "But I thank God, who always leads us in victory because of Christ. Wherever we go, God uses us to make clear what it means to know Christ. It's like a fragrance that fills the air." 2 Corinthians 2:14 (GW)

God is forever and will forever be our guide. "For this God is our God for ever and ever; he will be our guide even to the end." Psalm 48:14 (NIV)

When we are tempted to "awfulize" our situation, let's remember to not make our troubles or problems bigger than they are. Instead, let's turn our thoughts to thinking how big our God is in light of our problems.

BECOMING BRAVE

What is a sentence you sometimes catch yourself saying?

How can I _____?

There is no way _____.

I could never _____.

Take that same sentence and turn it around to become a positive one, adding something God has done for you at the end. Write it out below. It can look something like this:

Instead of *How can I get a good grade in math?*

You can say: *I can get a good grade in math because God has helped me before and He will help me again.*

Instead of *There is no way I could go to an overnight camp. I am too afraid.*

You could say: *I can go to an overnight camp, because God helped me when I stayed at Grandma's.*

Your turn:

_____

_____

_____

_____

COURAGEOUS CALL

Dear Jesus, I know I can exaggerate at times. Help me to start paying attention to my words and changing them for good. In Jesus' name, Amen.

CHAPTER 92

SAY IT

overcoming fear, speaking truth

It seemed to have come out of nowhere. Ryen was suddenly afraid of the dark. She felt afraid to go upstairs alone and never wanted her mom out of her sight. To tell you the truth, she felt a little bit funny having these fears overtake her. I'm 8 years old, she kept telling herself.

No matter what she tried, nothing seemed to work. Her mom began explaining to Ryen that the only person who could help her was Jesus. Her mom shared with her a story of a time when Jesus gave her the courage and strength to overcome something she had been afraid of. Ryen's mom knew Jesus would do the same for Ryen.

Together, Ryen and her mom made a plan. Ryen would pray

for courage and peace each time she started to feel scared. Even as she walked up each step to her bedroom, she'd repeat to herself or say out loud, "Jesus, be with me," "Jesus help me," or "Jesus protect me." Repeating these phrases helped Ryen find the peace in Jesus she needed to move forward.

At first, it felt pretty weird to Ryen, but she told her mom she would continue to give it a try. Going to Jesus with her fears didn't come naturally to Ryen, but she practiced leaning on Jesus for help. As she learned to seek and find his help to overcome her fears, she was beginning to gain his help in *all* areas of her life.

This idea of thinking good things then saying a prayer to overcome hard things is exactly what Philippians 4:8 (NIV) tells us to do: "Finally, brothers and sisters, whatever is true, whatever is noble, whatever is right, whatever is pure, whatever is lovely, whatever is admirable—if anything is excellent or praiseworthy—think about such things."

Why?

The "why" is told in the verses before verse 8: "Do not be anxious about anything, but in every situation, by prayer and petition, with thanksgiving, present your requests to God. And the peace of God, which transcends all understanding, will guard your hearts and your minds in Christ Jesus." Philippians 4:6–7 (NIV) When we choose to steer our minds toward things that are good and things we are thankful for, all the while telling God what we need, God's peace will come to us. That is exactly what Ryen needed: no fear and all of God's peace!

BECOMING BRAVE

To overcome her fears, Ryen is speaking good things about Jesus to her heart. What does your heart need you to say to it? Using the criteria of true, noble, right, pure, lovely, and admirable, write something you need to speak to your heart today.

_____

_____

_____

_____

COURAGEOUS CALL

Dear Jesus, thank you for writing things in the Bible that are so practical and help us to overcome our problems. In Jesus' name, Amen.

CHAPTER 93

THE LIST

self-esteem growing

As Jada looked in the mirror she thought, *I just don't get it. Why am I not growing yet?* So many of the girls in Jada's class were changing. It was as if she could see the changes daily! Some were getting taller—even taller than some of the boys. Others were experiencing changes in their bodies, making them look older. Not Jada. In fact, often when people guessed her age, they thought she was much younger. She was starting to get scared. *Will I ever change or am I going to look like a little girl for the rest of my life?*

The more she thought about it, the more worried she became. *Something is wrong with me* ran through her mind over and over again. She wanted to be done looking like a child. She wanted to look like the older girls at her school and the ones she saw on TV.

One day, Jada was brave enough to talk to her school nurse about her worries. The nurse helped her see the things about herself that Jada did like. She really liked her hair; it was such a pretty color. The nurse assured her there wasn't anything wrong with her. Her body was just taking a little extra time to grow. The nurse encouraged Jada to be kind to herself.

Jada found a piece of construction paper and made a list of all of the things she liked about herself. She took her list and put it in a pretty frame. Then, she hung it on the wall in her bedroom. Now, each time Jada sees her list, she is taking steps away from thinking about what she doesn't like about herself and seeing good instead.

Proverbs 23:7a (NKJV) tells us, "For as he thinks in his heart, so is he." The thoughts we think about ourselves are who we become. If I continually think negative thoughts about myself, I will become a person who feels bad about being me. If instead I turn my thoughts to thinking positively, I will become confident, strong, and secure.

BECOMING BRAVE

On any paper you choose make your own "Why I like me" list. Frame your list and hang it in a place where you can read it often.

COURAGEOUS CALL

Dear Jesus, it's hard not to compare myself to others. I know we are all different. Help me to speak to myself kindly and remember all the reasons it is great to be me. In Jesus' name, Amen.

CHAPTER 94

THE ANTICIPATION

heaven, faith, God's love

Planning a fun day is one of my favorite things to do, especially when that day is adventurous. You know what I enjoy almost as much as having an adventurous day? Planning it! It's fun getting books on our destination and looking for places and things to see, fun places to eat. Then, I create a schedule of our day. Before we leave our home, I write out what we will do.

For me, the anticipation is nearly as enjoyable as the day itself.

Planning and anticipating is something God and I have in common. While I plan special days, God is planning forever. He is having so much enjoyment creating a place for us to join Him one day. He gave us verses in the Bible that tell us about our ultimate destination so that we can experience the excitement of knowing we're heaven bound too.

Before Jesus left the earth, He said, "And if I go and prepare a place for you, I will come back and take you to be with me that you also may be where I am." John 14:3 (NIV)

That is exactly what He is doing, preparing a place for you and me so that we can be with Him one day.

Knowing that one day our destination is heaven gives us confidence. We know we are on this earth for a reason, to point others to Jesus. We also know that when our work here is all done, we will go on to live forever with Him in heaven. We do not have to fear when that time will come or how it will come. God loves us and He will keep us safe until that time comes.

So until it does, we can focus our energy and efforts away from fear and onto the faith we have in the one who is faithful to us!

GETTING TO KNOW YOU

(Circle one answer below each question.)

How often do you think about heaven?

a. Very often

b. Not very often

c. Rarely

If your answer was not very often or rarely, do you think that is because:

a. Those around you don't talk about it very often.

b. You don't know much about it.

c. It makes you uncomfortable.

What kind of "place" would you like God to prepare for you?

a. A palace.
b. A cabin.
c. A mansion.

COURAGEOUS CALL

Dear Jesus, I get excited when I think about heaven. Please bring thoughts of heaven to my mind so I can think often about the day when You and I are together forever. In Jesus' name, Amen.

CHAPTER 95

THE BRAVE GIRL REBEKAH

faith, scared, obedience

The Bible is full of stories about many brave people.

Genesis 24 tells the story of a courageous girl named Rebekah. You should read the whole tale.

Rebekah's story actually begins with Abraham, a father who needs to pick out a wife for his son. That is the way it was done in his country.

In the story, Abraham sent his servant to find Isaac a wife. Praying to God as he headed out, the servant trusted God to answer his prayer. When he stopped at a spring to get a drink of water, he asked God to show him if one of the girls coming to get water is the one for Isaac.

Before he even finished his prayer, Rebekah showed up. The servant thought, "This girl is the one I prayed for!" and he says to Rebekah, "Please give me a little water from your jar." She responded kindly, and the servant knew she was the wife for Isaac. Not only does Rebekah say yes to giving the servant a drink, she watered all of his camels too! Then she invited him to come and stay with her family for the night.

When the servant reached Rebekah's home, they discover they know each other's families. The servant shared the mission he was on: to find a wife for Isaac. They all agreed that God had brought them together to answer their prayers. Brave Rebekah said she would go back with the servant to become Isaac's wife.

Rebekah was so confident that God had His best for her that she bravely left her family to go where she had never been before to people she had never met! She courageously moved forward. She chose to fear less and have faith in God.

Hebrews 13:6 (NIV) tells us, "So we say with confidence, "The Lord is my helper; I will not be afraid. What can mere mortals do to me?" I would imagine Rebekah would have had feelings of fear, but she didn't allow those feelings to stop her from moving forward to what God had for her. May we be confident and brave like Rebekah!

BECOMING BRAVE

Sometimes when we have something new we need to do, we won't have all of the details. We might go somewhere we have never been or meet people we've never met before, like Rebekah. When you feel fearful of the unknown, remember Rebekah. Remember that God is your helper, just like Hebrews 13:6 says, and in Him you can fear less.

COURAGEOUS CALL

Dear God, build in me the confidence to go places I have never gone and meet people I have never met. Help me to remember Rebekah and choose to not fear. In Jesus' name, Amen.

CHAPTER 96

I DON'T BELONG HERE

heaven, salvation

Have you ever ridden on an airplane, bus, or train?

What if when you got on and sat down the lady next to you was making herself at home . . . literally. Curtains were hung on the window. Picture frames were displayed and her favorite trinkets were all around. The decorative blanket and pillow in her seat were the final touches.

Pretty weird, right? The vehicle is not her home—only the way to get her there.

This planet is not our home. Our bodies are just vehicles to take us to our heavenly home one day. Confidence comes from knowing this world is not our home. This world we live in is not permanent. Our bodies weren't made to last forever.

God didn't create us for here.

Paul tells it plainly in 2 Corinthians 5:1 (NIV), "For we know that if the earthly tent we live in is destroyed, we have a building from God, an eternal house in heaven, not built by human hands." Our home in heaven is built by the perfect Craftsman—God!

If there are times when I feel as if I don't fit here, I'm right! I don't and that is ok. I may be blessed to live a really long time (my grandma lived to be a 103 years old). In heaven though, I will live forever.

So, let's do the math. Based on how long we'll live here and how long we'll live there, what should we care more about?

Heaven!

Often, I don't remember that this world is not permanent. I get wrapped up in finding the right outfit or getting a project just right. When I base my confidence on what I can see, I can easily lose it. I can go to a party and wear the wrong thing. I can give my everything to a project and it still not go as planned. I can figure out every detail of my life, but something goes wrong. If I build my confidence on all these things, I'll lose it when they don't turn out.

If we build our confidence on the truth that what we have here is temporary, our hearts and minds won't get so worked up over our feats **or** our failures. They are only temporary anyway.

BECOMING BRAVE

Draw a picture of what you think our heavenly bodies will wear in heaven. What do you think the fashion will be there?

_____

_____

_____

_____

COURAGEOUS CALL

Dear Lord, it is a whole lot easier to base my confidence on what is going on here on earth because this is where I am living each day. When I feel discouraged, help me to remember, my time here on earth is not forever. This home is temporary. In Jesus' name, Amen.

CHAPTER 97

WHEN YOUR PARENTS DON'T FIT IN

being alone, bravery, changing, choices, family, fear of people, going against the crowd, growing up, loving difficult people, maturing, obedience, peer pressure, standing alone

Briana was so frustrated with her parents. Why did they have to be different from her friends' parents? Her friends got to do so many things Briana wasn't allowed to do. Apps, movies, popular songs—her parents had an opinion on everything. So many times what they felt was best for Briana and what Briana wanted weren't the same. She felt like she was the only one being told no.

It seemed to Briana that her friends were being allowed to grow up and make their own choices. Her parents were still making most of hers. She didn't get it and she didn't like it.

Feeling angry, Briana told her parents she wanted to do what everyone else got to do. She didn't want to be different. They shared with her that they are trying to teach her to live a Christ-centered life. And that life is sometimes going to be different from others.

This is what 1 Peter 2:9 (NIV) says about those who follow Christ: "But you are a chosen people, a royal priesthood, a holy nation, God's special possession, that you may declare the praises of him who called you out of darkness into his wonderful light."

When I was a young girl, I memorized this verse because I was struggling with being different. The translation I learned it in called those of us who love Jesus "a peculiar people." Peculiar means strange; queer; odd. That is how I sometimes felt compared to those who didn't follow Jesus.

When we make choices to honor God and when those choices are different from those around us, life can be frustrating. Often we can't see the reason or the positive consequences for obeying God. We have to trust that the hard decisions will pay off one day.

When you want to get from your kitchen to your bedroom, you take one step after another, right? The same is true in our lives. To be like Jesus, we take one step at a time in the right direction.

You may not be able to see the reason behind the choices your parents make. That's when you have to be mature and trust that your parents and God know what is best for you and hope that one day it will make sense.

BECOMING BRAVE

Write a play casting yourself as the parent and a friend as your child. Create a situation where the parent and child disagree. In the play, create conversation in which the parent gives the reasons for their answer. Do you like being the parent? Did it feel powerful to you or frustrating?

COURAGEOUS CALL

Dear Jesus, it is really hard for me to understand some of the decisions my parents make. Help me to respect them and remember that I may be a parent one day. Help me to treat them the way I want my child to treat me one day. In Jesus' name, Amen.

CHAPTER 98

NEEDING A LITTLE HELP

*being alone, growing up, changing, choices,
family, going against the crowd, maturing,
obedience, peer pressure, standing alone*

Reading my old diary recently, I came across this entry: "Went on a long walk with Mom and got advice." I remember doing that a lot with Mom. Growing up was hard and it helped me to be able to talk to someone who had already been there. Mom would remind me of what God's word said about my situation. (She knew the Bible so much better than I did.) She pointed me in the right direction, even if that direction was hard.

Sometimes, I needed help and Mom wasn't there—such as on the playground, when kids were using words I knew weren't right. At a friend's house, when a show came on TV that wasn't good for me to watch. In my classroom, when I was stuck on a problem and my neighbor's paper could easily be seen. I found myself needing advice and help at times when she couldn't be there to help me, couldn't be there to encourage me to be my best.

While going to Mom was a good thing, I have found I can always go to God. He is *always* there; nothing can hold him back from being by my side. Hebrews 4:16 (NIV) confirms that this is true: "Let us then approach God's throne of grace with confidence, so that we may receive mercy and find grace to help us in our time of need."

God doesn't expect us to be able to do everything on our own. He doesn't look down from heaven and think, *Is she ever going to get it right? Stop asking for my help all the time!* Instead, just as the verse says, we can confidently go to Him, knowing He wants to help us when we need Him most.

GETTING TO KNOW YOU

(*Circle one answer below each question.*)

How often do you ask God for help?

a. Many times during the day.

b. Once a day, during my normal prayers.

c. I don't really think about asking him to help me.

How do you think God feels when you ask for His help?

a. He feels like I am bugging him again.

b. He is happy that I am asking.

c. He doesn't care one way or another.

What can you do to help yourself get in the habit of asking God for help?

a. Begin to think of God as my friend.

b. Try talking to Him more than just during my normal times of prayer.

c. Wear something that reminds me to pray such as a bracelet or necklace.

COURAGEOUS CALL

Dear God, You are all powerful. I know that I need Your powerful help often during my day. Please remind me that when I need help, You are always there to help me and You want to. In Jesus' name, Amen.

CHAPTER 99

WHEN I FEEL LOST

being alone, bravery, going against the crowd,
fear of people, growing up, standing alone

The mall was jam packed for Christmas. Shoppers were rushing everywhere, trying to get their last minute gifts before the big day. Going to the mall with my mom was always fun. I especially liked knowing what she was buying my brothers and sisters before they knew what they were getting.

As the jingly music played, all the gorgeous decorations grabbed my eyes. The ceiling was so high and yet there were snowflakes and twinkly lights all the way to the top. **How did they get those there? Who put them up? Who took them down?**

When I finally stopped asking all of the questions in my mind, I looked around me. Where was Mom? Where had she gone? How long had I been standing there looking up while she had continued walking through the mall?

What was I going to do? I was lost!

Even today, I still remember that terrified feeling. I was in a huge place, surrounded by hundreds of people, none of whom I knew. I began to cry. I had no idea where to begin looking for my mom.

A mall worker saw me crying and asked me my name. Leading me to the store office, she sat me down and then called my mother's name over the loudspeaker. Soon, my mother was there. She hadn't gone anywhere; she was still right there in the same store. She wasn't mad at me or upset with me. She scooped me in her arms and gave me a huge hug!

Friend, there may be a time in your life when you feel like you've lost God. You haven't. He is there. Remember, God said: "Never will I leave you; never will I forsake you." Hebrews 13:5b. (NIV) You can never run too far from Him. He is always as near to you as your own breath.

BECOMING BRAVE

Maybe it has been years since you have played hide-and-go-seek or maybe it was yesterday! Either way, it's time to have fun again. Get a few friends together and play this old, but still fun game. As you take your turn hiding, remember: you can never hide from God and you can never be lost from Him either!

COURAGEOUS CALL

Dear God, there is no one I can count on like You. Others may leave me but You never, ever will. Thank you so much, Jesus! In Jesus' name, Amen.

I AM LOVED. I AM BRAVE.
I AM CONFIDENT.

brave, confident, loved, friendship, maturing

By ourselves, we don't naturally have confidence, courage, or bravery. When faced with a fearful situation or something that makes us uncomfortable, we might, in fact, fall apart.

During our time together, God has been forming confidence in us where we might not have had confidence before.

Just as God created the earth and everything in it out of nothing, God is creating something out of nothing in you and me. Psalm 33:6–9 (NIV) says, "By the word of the LORD the heavens were made, their starry host by the breath of his mouth. He gathers the waters of the sea into jars he puts the deep into storehouses. Let all the earth fear the LORD; let all the people of the world revere him. For he spoke, and it came to be; he commanded, and it stood firm."

According to Genesis 1 and Psalm 33:6–9, what does God use to create something out of nothing?

God uses his word. All He has to do is speak and it is done! This power that comes when He speaks, making something out of nothing, brought the sun shining through your window and the moon lighting up the night sky. His word also raised Jesus from the dead. This is the same power that can bring confidence into your life so that you can do all He has for you to do.

As my friend, Liz Curtis Higgs says, "When I feel weak, uncertain, vulnerable, the last thing I want is someone telling me, "Be strong!" That's like saying to spaghetti, "Stand up!" Even fresh out of the box, those dry, slender strands can't perch on end. But, when placed in the hands of a master chef, the spaghetti is easily held upright, secure in his grip." (http://www.lizcurtishiggs.com/the-20-verses-you-love-most-13-strong-and-brave/#sthash.eLGxFR5l.dpuf)

Friend, no matter what you face today and tomorrow, you are held upright, secure in your Father God's grip. He's got you and because He does, you can be confident.

BECOMING BRAVE

I hope that after reading this book and spending these 100 mini-chapters with God, you know you are loved, you are brave, and you are confident. Think of a friend you know who needs to also know she is loved, brave, and confident. Now, pass this book on to her.

COURAGEOUS CALL

Dear God, thank you for all You have taught me during this study. I pray that the truths I have learned in Your word will go deep in my heart so I never forget that in You I am loved, brave, and confident. In Jesus' name, Amen.

TOPICAL INDEX

About Proverbs 31 Ministries

If you were inspired by *Brave Beauty* and desire to deepen your own personal relationship with Jesus Christ, I encourage you to connect with Proverbs 31 Ministries.

Proverbs 31 Ministries exists to be a trusted friend who will take you by the hand and walk by your side, leading you one step closer to the heart of God through:

Free online daily devotions
First 5 Bible study app
Daily radio program
Books and resources
Online Bible Studies
COMPEL Writers Training: www.CompelTraining.com

To learn more about Proverbs 31 Ministries
call 1-877-731-4663 or visit www.Proverbs31.org.

Proverbs 31 Ministries
630 Team Rd., Suite 100
Matthews, NC 28105

www.Proverbs31.org